THE ZEN KOAN

THE
ZEN KOAN

ITS HISTORY AND USE IN RINZAI ZEN

ISSHŪ MIURA
RUTH FULLER SASAKI

With Reproductions of Ten Drawings
by Hakuin Ekaku

A Harvest/HBJ Book
A Helen and Kurt Wolff Book
Harcourt Brace Jovanovich, Publishers
San Diego New York London

ISBN   0-15-699981-1

Library of Congress Catalog Card Number: 65-19104

Printed in the United States of America

   KLMN

CONTENTS

vii

FOREWORD

THE First Zen Institute of America, founded in New York City in 1930 by the late SASAKI Sōkei-an Rōshi for the purpose of instructing American students of Zen in the traditional manner, celebrated its twenty-fifth anniversary on February 15, 1955. To commemorate that event it invited MIURA Isshū Rōshi of the Kōon-ji, a monastery belonging to the Nanzen-ji branch of Rinzai Zen and situated not far from Tokyo, to come to New York and give a series of talks at the Institute on the subject of koan study, the study which is basic for monks and laymen in traditional, transmitted Rinzai Zen.

Isshū Rōshi, though he spoke no English, was well qualified to deliver such a series of talks. At the age of ten he had become the personal disciple of SEIGO Hōgaku Rōshi, one of heirs of the famous Zen master SHAKU Sōen of the Engaku-ji, Kamakura. In his early twenties he entered the monastery of the Nanzen-ji in Kyoto. For twelve years he studied and practiced there under the stern stick of Nanshinken Rōshi. On the death of his master, he followed NAKAMURA Taiyū Rōshi, Nanshin-ken's heir, to the Kōon-ji. Two years later he completed his Zen study under Taiyū Rōshi. During the nine years that followed he successively held the position of priest of two important Zen temples; then, at the request of Taiyū Rōshi who was retiring, he returned to the Kōon-ji to become master of that monastery, a position he continues to hold, though at present teaching independently in New York.

The eight talks which Isshū Rōshi gave in New York had as their subject the system of koan study at present in use in all the Rinzai monasteries in Japan. This system was originated by Hakuin Ekaku (1686–1769), the reorganizer and revivifier of Japanese Rinzai Zen, and was further developed by his immediate disciples. Isshū Rōshi delivered these talks in Japanese; at the conclusion of each, an English translation was read which had been made by myself from the Rōshi's previously prepared manuscript. The success of these talks and the fact that a like treatment of their subject had never appeared in print in any western language led to plans for their publication in English. The unfamiliarity of the general reader with the subject seemed to demand some further treatment of it, however. As an introduction, therefore, an essay on the history of the origin and use of the koan by Chinese Ch'an masters and its further development by their heirs, the Rinzai masters of Japan, forms the first part of the present work.

With very few exceptions the books on Zen that have appeared in English or other western languages, even when they have made mention of the koan, have handled this important Zen teaching device superficially or mistakenly. This is in large part due to the fact that few westerners have thus far studied any koans at all, and only two to my knowledge have completed the study as outlined in Isshū Rōshi's talks. Koan study is a unique method of religious practice which has as its aim the bringing of the student to direct, intuitive realization of Reality without recourse to the mediation of words or concepts. In other words, its aim is that of all Buddhism since the time of Shakyamuni Buddha himself.

Two schools of Zen arose in China, the Ts'ao-tung (Sōtō) and the Lin-chi (Rinzai). In the former, the use of the koan took a secondary place, first place being assigned to the practice of *zazen*, or meditation as practiced in Zen. In the Lin-chi school, both zazen and the koan were considered of equal importance. Ts'ao-tung (Sōtō) and Lin-chi (Rinzai) Zen, when they were transmitted to Japan, brought with them these individual characteristics. Japanese Sōtō Zen continues to consider the practice of zazen to be the sole means of realization. It has never, however, discarded the koan, though employing it in its own way. Sōtō masters lecture on koans and their students study koans outside their practice of zazen.

The method of Rinzai Zen is different. In this school, zazen is, first of all, the preliminary practice by means of which mind and body are forged into a single instrument for realization. Only the student who has achieved some competency in zazen practice is, or should be, permitted to undertake the study of a koan. Proficiency in zazen is the basic ground for koan study. During the practice of zazen the koan is handled. To say that it is used as a subject of meditation is to state the fact incorrectly. The koan is taken over by the prepared instrument, and, when a fusion of instrument and device takes place, the state of consciousness is achieved which it is the intent of the koan to illumine and in this instant the koan is resolved. This experience may take place during formal zazen practice; it may as well be under any condition and at any time of the day or night. The experienced practicer of zazen does not depend upon sitting in quietude on his cushion. States of consciousness at first attained only in the meditation hall gradually become continuous, regardless of what other activities may be being engaged in.

The koan is not a conundrum to be solved by a nimble wit. It is not a verbal psychiatric device for shocking the disintegrated ego of a student into some kind of stability. Nor, in my opinion, is it ever a paradoxical statement except to those who view it from outside. When the koan is resolved it is realized to be a simple and clear statement made from the state of consciousness which it has helped to awaken. The course of koan study as devised by Hakuin Zenji from the koans of the old Chinese masters brings the student by degrees from the first awakening to Reality, the Principle, Absolute Mind, into full realization and oneness with the Absolute Principle in all manifestations of ITS activity, whether these be beyond time and space or in the humblest acts of daily life.

Those who would study Rinzai Zen would be well advised to inform themselves to some degree about the doctrines of developed Mahayana Buddhism on which all Zen is based, so that they may have at least a superficial acquaintance with the world they are about to enter. During the early period of koan study, they should dispense with all written words. Later, however, they will find the scriptures and writings of the masters to be only statements of what they themselves have already realized.

For the ordinary man busy with the affairs of everyday life, the lectures and writings of Zen men of attainment will be found to provide a degree of religious nourishment. Would that more were available! Japanese Zen offers him further insights through having infused into various realms of art expression certain intuitions attained through true Zen practice. But he who would plumb Zen and Buddhism to the depths must be a dedicated man, whether monk or layman. Fortunately the teaching and practice of all schools of Zen have always been open to both.

"THE HISTORY OF THE KOAN IN RINZAI (LIN-CHI) ZEN" is an attempt to provide the reader with a preliminary survey of the koan, its origin, history, and use. The deficiencies and inadequacies of this survey will be immediately apparent, as will the tentative nature of many of the statements in it. In spite of the mass of existing Chinese and Japanese Zen literature, there is little available on which to draw for such a study, and no modern Japanese or Chinese writer has thus far treated the koan from this standpoint. Particularly difficult to answer satisfactorily is the question of how the koan was used throughout the history of Zen, up to and even including the time of Hakuin and his disciples. The Zen masters have all remained disappointingly silent on this point, and we have only scattered hints in their writings to rely on.

The reader may find some difficulty in making the transition from the English style of "THE HISTORY OF THE KOAN" to that of the translation of Isshū Rōshi's text. The difference in style is due, in part at least, to the different standpoints from which the two texts approach koan study. "THE HISTORY OF THE KOAN" aims at being an objective, factual approach; Isshū Rōshi's approach is that of one who is within the actual practice itself. For the westerner who either is studying Zen or hopes to study it, this second approach is of the utmost importance. While we are standing outside Zen we must look at it clearly and cooly, as a fact in history; when we are "within" Zen we must give ourselves over to it completely if we are to experience that with which it is concerned. The two standpoints should not be confused; rather, they must be carefully differentiated.

No attention has previously, I believe, been given to the use of *jakugo*, or "capping phrases," in Rinzai Zen koan study. Their purpose is explained in "THE HISTORY OF THE KOAN." A section devoted to translated excerpts from *Zenrin kushū*, the anthology of quotations in which the majority of accepted jakugo are to be found, forms PART THREE of this work. Since the Japanese reading of the Chinese text of these phrases is often special for Zen, these readings and the Chinese character text have been included for the interest they may have to students.

Since the subject proper of *THE ZEN KOAN* is Hakuin Ekaku's system of koan study and since long quotations from his writings comprise a part of Isshū Rōshi's text, that great master is in a sense the hero of this book. No work in which Hakuin appears would be complete without some examples of his painting and calligraphy. Hakuin was not a painter in the professional sense of the term; he was a Zen master who used his great talent as an artist in teaching Zen, particularly to his lay followers. Thanks to the extreme kindness and courtesy of the Marquis HOSOKAWA Moritatsu, who studied at the monastery of the Daitoku-ji in his youth and whose interest in Zen has continued unfailingly through half a century, it has been possible to include in *THE ZEN KOAN* a number of Hakuin's drawings, all from the Marquis' famous collection. Every writer on Japanese Zen is faced with the problem of how to deal with Chinese proper names and Chinese Buddhist (or Zen) technical terms, for no book on Japanese Zen can be written without constant reference to the old Chinese masters, the places where they lived, the books they wrote, or the special words they used. Unfortunate though it may be, for the time at least, the study of Zen history and literature as well as the practice of Zen itself can best be pursued in Japan. Japanese Buddhist scholars, even when they are acquainted with Chinese, tend to use only Japanese pronunciation for Chinese names and terms; the Japanese Zen masters use nothing else. Westerners studying in Japan must of necessity conform to the Japanese custom in speaking, but accuracy demands that, in writing, names and terms (when not translated) be rendered in the language of their origin. Thus the western student has no alternative but to familiarize himself thoroughly with both pronunciations.

Probably no method of handling this problem of dual pronunciation is totally satisfactory. The present book makes no claim to have offered a solution of the problem or even to have been consistent throughout in the method used. In PART ONE, Chinese names with the Chinese characters for them have been given for Chinese people, places, and so forth. When such a name (or word) is immediately followed by another name (or word) in parenthesis, the latter may be assumed to be the Japanese pronunciation of the former. When a name or word is not followed by a parenthesis, it may be assumed that its origin is Japanese. An exception to this rule has been made in Isshū Rōshi's text. There, the Japanese pronunciation has been used throughout for all names and terms, regardless of whether they were originally Chinese of Japanese. This has been done in order not to disturb the sense of participating in a Japanese roshi's lecture or interrupt the flow of the text. In every case, the INDEX will be found to supply the Chinese characters and pronunciations lacking in the text. The names of Japanese and Chinese persons are given with the family name first and the personal name following; capitalization clearly establishes the order. The names of Chinese and Japanese Buddhist priests are given in the order most usually accepted in Japanese Buddhism. The problem of the anglicization of words also presents itself. The word "Zen" has now become all but standard English for the name of this school of Buddhism as a whole, and is so used here. The Chinese equivalent "Ch'an" has, however, been employed when a subject is being handled from the Chinese standpoint specifically, or to make a clear distinction between the Chinese and Japanese schools. There are, in addition, a number of words, such as *rōshi, sōdō, kenshō,* which it seems advisable to anglicize eventually in their Japanese pronunciation, since the English language provides no exact equivalent for them and since these words must be an integral part of the daily vocabulary of the Zen scholar or the practicing Zen student. When these first appear in this text they are given in italics in Japanese romanized form with proper markings; thereafter they are used as English words.

Two technical terms of great importance in Zen have also been used as English words in THE ZEN KOAN. The Chinese word *tao,* in Japanese *dō,* is one of several terms which the early Chinese Buddhists took over from Taoism. In Chinese Buddhism the term *tao* sometimes means "the Way," that is, the Eightfold Path of the Buddha, or the "way" leading to enlightenment; sometimes it means enlightenment itself, sometimes Nirvana. In Zen, however, its meaning is more closely akin to that in Taoism; it is the Absolute, the Ultimate Principle, Truth, Reason, the indescribable source of all existence and all manifested phenomena. Since western philosophical and religious thought has not developed the concepts embedded within and clinging to this Chinese word, no equivalent term exists in the English language. Moreover, to translate it by a single English word, though that might be appropriate in a given context, is to permit western associative concepts to blot out the original Chinese overtones. Therefore it would seem preferable to treat the word "Tao" as an adopted word in English, thus permitting it gradually to acquire for the English reader the meanings and shades of meaning rightfully belonging to it. The word has thus been used wherever it appears in this text, leaving the reader to feel into it whatever the context implies.

The Sanskrit word *dharma*, in Chinese *fa*, and in Japanese pronounced *hō*, also is the product of the specific culture and thought of the country of its origin, and no one word in any European language can contain its many and varied meanings. It is now an accepted word in English and has found a place in recent English dictionaries. As a technical term in Hinduism, the meanings of the word "dharma" vary greatly from those it has acquired as a Buddhist technical term. In this later usage, which alone concerns us, it has two distinct meanings: firstly, Law, Truth, religion, the doctrines and teachings of the Buddha, Buddhism; secondly, the elements of existence, things, phenomena. In order not to confuse the reader, it would seem helpful to write the term "Dharma" when it is used with any one of the meanings in the first group; and, when it is used with any one of the meanings in the second group, to write it "dharma" or "dharmas." This rule has been used throughout in *THE ZEN KOAN*.

Though only the names of Isshū Rōshi and myself appear on the title page of *THE ZEN KOAN*, the book is actually the work of a happy collaboration in which several persons have joined. Thanks are first offered to the late GOTŌ Zuigan Rōshi, former Chief Abbot of Myōshin-ji and of Daitoku-ji, for his guidance in the rendering of the Japanese readings of the *Zenrin kushū* excerpts and his painstaking explanation of the meanings read into them in Zen, from which certain of the English translations have profited. To all the members of the Research Staff of the First Zen Institute of America in Japan we are indebted for their cooperation, but especially to Professor Yoshitaka IRIYA, Head of the Department of Chinese Literature, Nagoya University, and our Director of Research, who has been our instructor and guiding hand throughout, and to Mr. Philip YAMPOLSKY and Dr. Burton WATSON, former members of the

Staff, who were of great assistance while they were with us. However, all errors of fact or interpretation as well as inaccuracies in the English rendering of translated material are my own.

In conclusion, The First Zen Institute of America in Japan wishes to express its gratitude to the Bollingen Foundation, New York, for its generous grant toward the preparation and publication of *THE ZEN KOAN*.

RUTH FULLER SASAKI

Ryōsen-an
Daitoku-ji
January 1, 1965

PART ONE

THE HISTORY OF THE KOAN
IN RINZAI (LIN-CHI) ZEN

I. THE KOAN IN CHINESE ZEN

THE living heart of all Buddhism is enlightenment or satori, and it is upon satori that Zen Buddhism is based. But Zen is not satori, nor is satori Zen. Satori is the goal of Zen. Moreover, the satori that is the goal of Zen is not merely the satori experience; it is the satori experience deepened through train ing and directed to a definite end.

The state of satori is outside of time. The training before and after satori is within time. The masters who devised the methods of training used in Zen were men living in given environments in given periods of history; their personalities and those of their students, to say nothing of their attitudes, actions, and speech, were in part determined by the times and the cultures in which they lived. The teaching methods of the earliest days have undergone much modification through the centuries. In the future, in Japan as well as in the West— when and if real Zen does go West—the present forms of the traditional methods will undoubtedly be still further modified.

3

The principles and aims of the Zen masters cannot be said to have changed, however. When these are changed, there will no longer be any Zen.

Zen makes use of three kinds of training in bringing its followers to the experience of satori and maturing that experience: meditation or zazen, the study of koans, and daily life. The Zen manner of employing meditation and daily life is distinctive, but the koan and the methods of using it are unique and to be found in Zen alone. It is with a short survey of the koan and its use as they developed in history, particularly with reference to the school of Zen known in China as the Lin-chi 臨濟, and in Japan as the Rinzai, that we shall be concerned here.

There is no need to consider the misinformation being spread about the koan by those professed exponents of Zen in the West who have never studied koans themselves. The Zen masters have stated quite clearly what a koan is and for what purpose it is used. One of the best of these statements is to be found in the *Chung-fêng ho-shang kuang-lu*, the "record" of the Lin-chi master Chung-fêng Ming-pên 中峰明本 (Chūhō Myōhon, 1263–1323), who lived during the Yüan 元 (Gen) dynasty (1260–1368). When he was asked why the teachings of the buddhas and patriarchs were called "public records," that is, koans, he replied:

The koans may be compared to the case records of the public law court. Whether or not the ruler succeeds in bringing order to his realm depends in essence upon the existence of law. *Kung* 公 (*kō*), or "public," is the single track followed by all sages and worthy men alike, the highest principle which serves as a road for the whole world. *An* 案 (*an*), or "records," are the orthodox writings which record what the sages and worthy men regard as principles. There have never been rulers who did not have public law courts, and there have never been public law courts that did not have case records which are to be used as precedents of laws in order to stamp out injustice in

4

the world. When these public case records (koans) are used, then principles and laws will come into effect; when these come into effect, the world will become upright; when the world is upright, the Kingly Way will be well ordered.

Now, when we use the word "koan" to refer to the teachings of the buddhas and patriarchs, we mean the same thing. The koans do not represent the private opinion of a single man, but rather the highest principle, received alike by us and by the hundreds and thousands of bodhisattvas of the three realms and the ten directions. This principle accords with the spiritual source, tallies with the mysterious meaning, destroys birth-and-death, and transcends the passions. It cannot be understood by logic; it cannot be transmitted in words; it cannot be explained in writing; it cannot be measured by reason. It is like the poisoned drum that kills all who hear it, or like a great fire that consumes all who come near it. What is called the "special transmission of the Vulture Peak" was the transmission of this; what is called the "direct pointing of Bodhidharma at Shao-lin-ssu" was a pointing at this.

. . . .

From the time long ago when the lotus flower was held up on the Vulture Peak until today, how can there have been only seventeen hundred koans? Yet the koans are something that can be used only by men with enlightened minds who wish to prove their understanding. They are certainly not intended to be used merely to increase one's lore and provide topics for idle discussion.

The so-called venerable masters of Zen are the chief officials of the public law courts of the monastic community, as it were, and their words on the transmission of Zen and their collections of sayings are the case records of points that have been vigorously advocated. Occasionally men of former times, in the intervals when they were not teaching, in spare moments when their doors were closed, would take up these case records and arrange them, give their judgment on them, compose verses of praise on them, and write their own answers to them. Surely they did not do this just to show off their erudition and contradict the worthy men of old. Rather, they did it because they could not bear to think that the Great Dharma might become corrupt. Therefore they stooped to using expedients in order to open up the Wisdom Eye of the men of later generations, hoping thereby to make it possible for them to attain the understanding of the Great Dharma for themselves in the same way. That is all.

The word *kung*, or "public," means that the koans put a stop to private understanding; the word *an*, or "case records," means that they are guaranteed to accord with the buddhas and patriarchs. When these koans are understood and accepted, then there will be an end to feeling and discrimination; when there is an end to feeling and discrimination, birth-and-death will become empty; when birth-and-death becomes empty, the Buddha-way will be ordered.

What do I mean by according with the buddhas and patriarchs? The buddhas and patriarchs have been greatly sorrowed to see that sentient beings bind themselves to the realm of birth-and-death and sensual delusion, so that, through the countless kalpas of the past down to the present, none have been able to free themselves. Therefore they displayed words in the midst of wordlessness and handed down forms in the midst of formlessness. But once the bonds of delusion have been loosed, how can there be any words and forms left to discuss?

If an ordinary man has some matter which he is not able to settle by himself, he will go to the public law court to seek a decision, and there the officials will look up the case records and, on the basis of them, settle the matter for him. In the same way, if a student has that in his understanding of his enlightenment which he cannot settle for himself, he will ask his teacher about it, and the teacher, on the basis of the koans, will settle it for him.

The koan is a torch of wisdom that lights up the darkness of feeling and discrimination, a golden scraper that cuts away the film clouding the eye, a sharp ax that severs the root of birth-and-death, a divine mirror that reflects the original face of both the sacred and the secular. Through it the intention of the patriarchs is made abundantly clear, the Buddha-mind is laid open and revealed. For the essentials of complete transcendence, final emancipation, total penetration, and identical attainment, nothing can surpass the koan.

The origin of the koan and the method of using it lie in the nature of Zen itself. The masters of earliest Zen discerned that the source of the dynamic power of Buddhism was not in the sutras and the voluminous commentaries upon them, but in the enlightenment of Shakyamuni and in his teaching that every man has the potentiality of attaining this enlightenment for himself. Supported by faith in this teaching, these early masters forged ahead with indomitable courage to gain this realization for themselves through the method Shakyamuni had used and advocated, that is, meditation. Having attained the realization and comprehended its deepest meaning as well as its implications for human life, out of the compassionate heart born of their enlightenment they sought ways and means of assisting others to achieve the same experience. Meditation certainly remained the basic practice. Though methods of meditation were developed in Zen that differed from those in other Buddhist sects, whether of Indian or Chinese origin, we have no evidence that meditation itself was ever abandoned or even neglected. Nor is it neglected today. The different schools of Zen developed somewhat different ways of handling the mind during meditation, but in all schools the main road to the attainment of satori is still that of practicing meditation in the posture in which Shakyamuni Buddha was sitting when he attained his enlightenment.

The earliest Chinese masters seem to have attained their enlightenment with little instruction. The histories of their

7

lives indicate that most had been Buddhist monks, many from a young age, and as such were steeped in the doctrines of the Buddhist scriptures. Many had studied the classics of Confucianism and Taoism as well. Their inability to attain the enlightenment they sought through the study of written words caused them to seek out meditation masters. When these monks had reached some profound insight through their meditation practice they went to the master to have their insight verified by his. Or, if they were beset by doubts, they went to him to have these doubts resolved. Many times the master's one word at this point brought them to satori. If the master seemed to be *their* master, they remained with him for a number of years; if not, they went on to other masters until they found the one they recognized to be their own. When their enlightenment had been attested to and confirmed, they retired to the mountains to spend long years in ripening it. Only gradually did other seekers find them out and come to live with or near them. From such a group a new temple might arise, or, if the master's fame had reached the capital, a command might come to take charge of one already established.

The satori or enlightenment that the old masters experienced was ineffable and incommunicable. It had not come about as the result of thinking or reasoning. It was, indeed, an experience beyond and above the intellect. Understanding this only too well, they did not, on the whole, attempt to describe their experiences in words. They knew that verbal explanations were useless as a means of leading their students to the realization itself. They had to devise other means.

In the mountain monasteries where they preferred to live, the early Chinese masters were in intimate contact with their disciples, sharing all phases of their daily life and work. While master and monks were picking tea, planting trees, or sitting around the fire together, the master, by means of a seemingly simple question about something in the immediate situation, would indicate to the disciple some aspect of the immutable Principle, bringing him to a deeper realization, or test the depth of understanding he had already achieved.

From time to time the masters took the high seat in the main hall of the monastery and gave lectures to the assembly of monks. On such occasions they did not expound the sutras or scriptures as did the clerics of other sects of Buddhism. Though, on the whole, Zen masters were conversant with the teachings of other schools—and many of these teachings undoubtedly underlie Zen thought and doctrines—from the first Zen had prided itself on *not* being founded on any scripture. Zen was concerned only with Absolute Mind. Absolute Mind was the masters' one theme, pure, original, basic Mind, and their every word and action was a pointing to and a manifesting of Absolute Mind. In energetic and vivid language, much of it the colloquial idiom of the time, interspersed with quotations from the sutras and other Buddhist writings, the old masters relentlessly drove their message home. When they gave their own views, these were apt to be expressed in cryptic statements and formulas. At such times members of the community and any visiting monks and laymen who might be present were free to ask the master for further elucidation. They were also free to ask him questions of their own, or to bring up one of the numerous stereotyped questions that Zen adherents seemed always to have at hand when they had nothing else to inquire about.

The master took advantage of all such opportunities to demonstrate the Principle, to awaken the questioner to deeper levels of understanding, or to destroy his pretensions. The answer the master gave, whether in word or in action, though always pointing to the Principle, was invariably adapted to the particular occasion. Thus it often came about that at different times the same master gave different answers to the same question. Furthermore, since these early masters were men of great originality and creative ability, their ways of demonstrating the profound Principle, their questions, and even their answers to the stock questions asked them, invariably bore the stamp of their own individual genius.

As the number of students around the famous masters grew larger, the personal contacts of the earlier days could not be maintained except with immediate disciples. Then a master might give to a number of students a certain question that he had already found effectual. Though the question originally had arisen in response to an immediate situation and was the immediate and personal problem of the individual disciple to whom it had been addressed, since the principle the master was making manifest through it was the immutable Principle and therefore valid for all men, the question also was valid for other students. Such questions performed the function of koans, and there is some evidence that by the end of T'ang (618–907) the masters themselves were referring to them as koans. But they were not koans in the full sense of the word, for they were questions being used by the masters who had originally created them. However, when Nan-yüan Hui-yung 南院慧顒 (Nan'in Egyō, *d*. 930), a descendant of Lin-chi I-hsüan 臨濟義玄 (Rinzai Gigen, *d*. 866) in the 3rd generation, questioned a disciple about certain of Lin-chi's formulas, Koan Zen, or the use of the words of earlier masters in a fixed and systematized form to instruct or test a student, may be said to have truly begun.

From that time on, the most illustrious masters, though they did not entirely cease creating their own koans, depended in large part on the "words of the ancients" in instructing their students, and the less talented masters relied upon them entirely. We may suppose that there were at least two reasons for this: the decline in the high level of creative genius with which the earlier masters had been endowed, and the great increase in the number, with a corresponding decrease in the quality, of the monks and lay students who were now flocking to individual monasteries by the hundreds, even thousands, to be instructed by the more reputable masters.

What were the "words of the ancients" now being used as "public records" or koans? Briefly, they consisted of questions the early masters had asked individual students, together with the answers given by the students; questions put to the masters by students in personal talks or in the course of the masters' lectures, together with the masters' answers; statements of formulas in which the masters had pointed to the profound Principle; anecdotes from the daily life of the masters in which their attitudes or actions illustrated the functioning of the Principle; and occasionally a phrase from a sutra in which the Principle or some aspect of it was crystallized in words. By presenting a student with one or another of these koans and observing his reaction to it, the degree or depth of his realization could be judged. The koans were the criteria of attainment.

Thus a unique method had been evolved for assisting men to attain religious awakening, a method of teaching in which there was no stated creed to be believed or precepts to be followed, no instruction in doctrines or discussions about them, no wordy descriptions of the stages on the way to enlightenment. Nor did the masters examine their students by asking them to state their views and beliefs in words. The koan was the examination. If the student had attained the understanding of the Principle as embodied in the koan, he would reply in such a fashion as clearly to indicate this. If not, then he must take the koan and wrestle with it, in the meditation hall and in the course of carrying out his daily tasks, until such time as he and it became one. The master gave him no further help or instruction.

But there was one serious weakness in this system that early began to be apparent. When the master picked up something right before the student's eye and used it to instruct him, the realization of this very thing as the manifestation or functioning of the Principle was the disciple's own and immediate problem. There was neither time nor opportunity to consider. Here stood the master towering above him demanding right then and there an immediate response. Of course the student might, and often did, fail to respond satisfactorily. But even then the problem remained his own, personal, immediate, and vital problem to solve, and to solve as quickly as possible if he was to have any peace of mind. But when many koans had been written down and he could read them at his leisure, or he had heard them stated many times and their possible or probable meanings discussed, the immediacy to him of even one koan, let alone hundreds, became difficult to feel. It became easy to give in to thinking about them, to comparing those of one master with those of another, to considering them in their historical setting, to enjoying them as literary curiosities. This tendency to handle the koan intellectually has been a persistent problem throughout the history of Koan Zen, and still remains one today.

Collections of "old cases," as the koans were sometimes called, as well as attempts to put the koans into a fixed form and to systematize them to some extent, were already being made by the middle of the 10th century. We also find a few masters giving their own alternate answers to some of the old koans and occasionally appending verses to them. In many cases these "alternate answers" and verses ultimately became attached to the original koans and were handled as koans supplementary to them.

The Lin-chi master Fên-yang Shan-chao 汾陽善昭 (Fun'yō Zenshō, 947–1024) was the first to employ all these various trends. His "record," the *Fên-yang Wu-tê ch'an-shih yü-lu*, includes three collections of one hundred koans each. The first collection consists of old koans, for each of which Fên-yang wrote a verse epitomizing the import of the koan in poetical language; the second consists of koans he himself had made and for which he provided his own answers; the third is made up of old koans, together with Fên-yang's alternate answers to them. These three collections became the models for later literary productions of a similar kind.

The most important of the collections of koans with attached verses was that made by Hsüeh-tou Ch'ung-hsien 雪竇重顯 (Setchō Jūken, 980–1052), a master of the Yün-mên 雲門 (Ummon) School, which was later absorbed by the Lin-chi School. Hsüeh-tou's *Po-tsê sung-ku* contained one hundred "old cases" favored in his teaching line, and included eighteen original koans by the famous founder of the school, Yün-mên Wên-yen 雲門文偃 (Ummon Bun'en, 862/4–949). Hsüeh-tou was not only an outstanding Zen master but a distinguished

12

poet of the time.

A century later the Lin-chi master Yüan-wu K'o-ch'in 圜悟克勤 (Engo Kokugon, 1063–1135) used Hsüeh-tou's collection as the basis for a series of lectures in which he commented not only upon the one hundred koans Hsüeh-tou had selected but on Hsüeh-tou's verses as well. Yüan-wu's lectures, recorded and compiled by his disciples, were soon issued under the title *Pi-yen lu*.

In Yüan-wu's time the intellectualistic tendencies in Koan Zen were already widespread. Men were reasoning and theorizing about the koans, comparing and memorizing them and their answers in large numbers, and writing verses and explanatory statements about them. Though Yüan-wu himself engaged in considerable literary activity, he was keenly aware of the dangers inherent in this trend, and spoke out sharply against it. He insisted, as had other masters before him from Yün-mên on, that it was through penetration into a few koans, or even into only one, that the attainment of true insight into Absolute Mind is achieved. "If you understand a single koan right now, you can clearly understand all the teachings of the ancients as well as those of the men of today," he stated.

It was during the lifetime of Yüan-wu's successor Ta-hui Tsung-kao 大慧宗杲 (Daie Sōkō, 1089–1163) that Koan Zen entered its determinative period. Ta-hui was a true heir of Yüan-wu. He vigorously opposed the literary and intellectual approach to the koan, and even went so far as to take violent measures to have his master's *Pi-yen lu* destroyed, feeling that the study of it was injurious to true Zen attainment. On the other hand, Ta-hui just as firmly advocated the right use of the old koans. The method he ceaselessly urged on his students was concentrated introspection of the koan, introspection into which not the slightest deliberation or intellectualization entered. The koan was to be introspected only, introspected deeper and deeper until its full content was revealed.

By Ta-hui's time, with the exception of the Ts'ao-tung 曹洞 (Sōtō) School, the various teaching lines of Zen that had originally stemmed from the disciples of the Sixth Patriarch had virtually all been absorbed into the Lin-chi School. The masters of the Ts'ao-tung School, while they used koans and made the usual collections of selected koans with verses and commentaries attached, tended to place more emphasis upon the practice of meditation. Now a famous controversy arose between Ta-hui and Hung-chih Chêng-chüeh 宏智正覺 (Wan-shi Shōgaku, 1091–1157), a leading master of the Ts'ao-tung School. Ta-hui upheld the introspection of the koan as the superior method for attaining satori, while Hung-chih advocated that satori be attained through sitting quietly and bringing the mind to a state of complete tranquillity and emptiness. Ta-hui was not against the correct practice of meditation or zazen, in fact he was strongly in favor of it. It was primarily in zazen that the koan was to be introspected. What Ta-hui was against was the adherence to a quietistic type of sitting that he felt could only result in passivity and lifelessness, never in the dynamic experience of true satori. And Hung-chih, however strongly he may have championed "silent-illumination" meditation, did not himself dispense with the koan. From this time on the Zen of the Lin-chi School came to be known as k'an-hua ch'an 看話禪 (kanna zen), or "introspecting-the-koan Zen," and the Zen of the Ts'ao-tung School as mo-chao ch'an 默照禪 (mokushō zen), or "silent-illumination Zen." Perhaps the controversy between the two masters was not so heated as it was later made to appear. Ta-hui and Hung-chih seem always to have been friends, and before his death Hung-chih entrusted the disposition of his affairs to Ta-hui. Nevertheless, later generations of adherents in both schools continued the argument with a fervor not always so free from rancor and virulence as it had originally been.

Throughout the Yüan dynasty and into the Ming (1368–1644), the masters of both schools carried on their literary activities uninterruptedly. It is ironic indeed that a school which was founded upon an experience above all words should have produced the vast amount of literature that Zen produced in China and later in Japan. But at no time in the history of Zen were the masters unaware of their basic aim or of the problems that faced them in accomplishing it. Whether the method they advocated for the attainment of satori was the introspection of koans or the practice of zazen only, the masters had but one sole purpose, that of assisting men to realize Absolute Mind for themselves. And their writings, voluminous as they undeniably were, were attempts to urge men on to this goal.

In what way the later Chinese masters instructed their students in the koans is not clear. Certainly they gave numerous lectures in commentary on the koans, and their disciples seem to have recorded these lectures more or less meticulously. But whether the masters used koans to question their students during or at the conclusion of their lectures, whether the students in groups or individually came to the masters freely or at stated times, whether the master gave the student the koan or whether the student chose a koan for himself and then went to the master to have his insight tested, we do not know with any certainty. In Ta-hui's writings we find some disparaging remarks about the "transmission in the secret room," but he gives us no clue as to what the "secret room" was. After the great influx of monks and lay students into the monasteries at the end of T'ang and the beginning of Sung (960–1279), the numbers of followers slowly decreased, but there must always have been large groups of disciples around the important masters. Presumably the masters continued to be in close contact with their immediate disciples and to use the opportunities offered in daily life to question and instruct them. This is as much as can at present be said about this aspect of koan study. Perhaps the future will see it further clarified.

The development of the koan method reached its apogee in China in the Sung dynasty. The masters of the Yüan still displayed some of the old virility, but by then Zen had already begun its long decline in China. During Ming, the Lin-chi School absorbed not only the Ts'ao-tung School, but all other schools of Chinese Buddhism as well, to say nothing of elements from Tibetan Tantric Buddhism, popular Taoism, and the native folk religion. Fully accepted in the Ch'an of the Ming dynasty were the *nien-fo* 念佛 (*nembutsu*) practices of the Pure Land School, which, having had a few advocates for a short period in the early days of Ch'an, from the beginning of the Yüan dyanasty had been gradually infiltrating it again. Though certain teachers in the direct lines of transmission from the masters of Sung and Yüan continued the traditional ways of teaching, they did so only with many adaptations to the new accretions and the changing times.

Modern Chinese Ch'an, about which we are only now beginning to know something, seems to be a development from the Ch'an of the Ming and Ch'ing (1644–1912) dynasties. Japanese Zen, as we shall see, had its roots in the Zen of Sung and early Yüan. The one line of Ming Zen that came to Japan had little or no direct influence upon the teaching or teaching methods already firmly established there in the Rinzai and Sōtō schools. In Japan today, therefore, in order to make a clear differentiation, Japanese Zen is often referred to as "Sung Zen," and modern Chinese Ch'an as "Ming Zen."

II. THE KOAN IN JAPANESE ZEN

ZEN was introduced into Japan at a very early date, but five centuries were to pass before conditions were ripe for it to take root. The first known meditation teacher in Japan was the Japanese monk Dōshō 道昭 (629–700), who went to China in 653 to study under the famous Buddhist scholar Hsüan-tsang 玄奘 (Genjō, 600?–664), and on his return to Japan taught meditation at a temple in Nara. In 736 the Chinese Commandment Master Tao-hsüan Lü-shih 道璿律師 (Dōsen Risshi, 702–760) arrived in Nara. There he propagated not only the teachings of the Commandment or Vinaya Sect (Risshū 律宗 Lü-tsung) but also those of the Kegon Sect 華嚴宗 (Hua-yen-tsung) and those of the Northern School of Zen as well. Tao-hsüan's Japanese heir Gyōhyō 行表 (722–797) is said to have taught the meditation of this school of Zen to the Japanese Tendai 天台 monk Saichō 最澄 (767–822). Later, Saichō went to China and studied at T'ien-t'ai-shan 天台 山 (Tendaizan). While he was there he was given the T'ien-

17

t'ai (Tendai) ordination and, in addition, received instruction from Vinaya, Ch'an (Zen), and Chên-yen 眞言 (Shingon) masters. After he had returned to Japan and founded the Japanese Tendai Sect on Mount Hiei 比叡山 near Kyoto, Dengyō Daishi 傳教大師, the posthumous title by which Saichō is better known, included the practices of all these schools in his teaching. The last of the early Zen teachers was I-k'ung 義空 (Gikū, *n.d.*), a master of the Southern School of Zen who came to Kyoto in the middle of the 9th century at the invitation of the Empress-Consort Danrin 檀林 (787–851). Although I-k'ung was under the patronage of the Court, his teaching had little success, and a few years later he returned to China. For the next three centuries the power of the Tendai and Shingon sects was such that no other Buddhist school could gain a foothold in Japan.

Over three hundred years later the Tendai monk Myōan Eisai 明庵榮西 (1141–1215), during his second trip to China, studied under a Lin-chi master and received the Seal of Transmission. After his return to Kyoto, he founded there in 1202 the temple known as the Kennin-ji 建仁寺, the first Zen temple to be established in Kyoto. Eisai introduced the teaching of Rinzai Zen at the Kennin-ji, but even at this late period he found it necessary to include with it Shingon and Tendai practices.

Eisai's successor at the Kennin-ji was Ryōnen Myōzen 了然 明全 (1184–1225). Among Myōzen's students was a young monk, Dōgen Kigen 道元希玄 (1200–1253), who had become discouraged with his Tendai studies on Mount Hiei. Dōgen was eager to go to China, and urged Myōzen to accompany him. In 1223 master and disciple set forth on their voyage. During their stay in China Myōzen died, but Dōgen remained on, continuing his Zen practice under the Sōtō 曹洞 (Ts'ao-tung) master T'ien-t'ung Ju-ching 天童如浄 (Tendō Nyojō, 1163–1228) until he had received the Seal of Transmission. T'ien-t'ung, though he is known to have used certain koans in his teaching, was one of the most outspoken opponents of the Kanna Zen ("introspecting-the-koan Zen") of the Lin-chi School. His attitude in this respect and its influence upon his Japanese disciple was a determining factor in the course that Sōtō Zen was to follow in Japan through all the long years to come. Dōgen returned to Japan in 1227. Though an aristocrat by birth, from the first he avoided any contact with either the Imperial Court at Kyoto or the Shogunate in Kamakura. He had no wish to found a school; he desired only to live quietly in a small temple, devoting himself to the realization of the truths of Buddhism through meditation and daily life. But students, both monks and laymen, were soon coming to him. As their numbers increased, he moved from one country temple to another. In 1245 the great monastery of Eihei-ji 永平寺, built for him by his disciples in the mountains of Echizen 越前, in present-day Fukui Prefecture, was completed. Dōgen had now become the deeply revered founder of the sect of Japanese Sōtō Zen.

Dōgen's Zen was centered in zazen. The meditation practice which he vigorously affirmed was that known as *shikan taza* 祇管打坐, "zazen only." "Zazen is the Buddha-dharma and the Buddha-dharma is zazen," he wrote in his great work *Shōbōgenzō*. Nevertheless Dōgen did not reject koans; like his master before him, he seems to have used them in instructing his immediate disciples. Under Keizan Jōkin 瑩山 紹瑾 (1268–1325), fourth patriarch of the sect, the koan was completely discarded, in theory at least, and zealous efforts were made to give Japanese Sōtō Zen a widespread and popular appeal. Nevertheless, the study of koans and of the koan collections of the Sōtō masters of Sung has continued to play an important part in Sōtō training, though undoubtedly the masters of the sect have handled this teaching device in a somewhat different manner than have the masters of Japanese Rinzai Zen.

Only two Chinese Sōtō masters, descendants of Hung-chih Chêng-chüeh in the 6th and 7th generations, are recorded to have journeyed to Japan, one in 1309 and the other in 1351. Both taught their style of Zen at various Rinzai temples in Japan, and both founded teaching lines that soon became extinct. They seem to have made no contact with the Japanese branch of their own sect. Japanese Sōtō Zen, despite the adaptations to Japanese life and culture made in it by its later patriarchs, has always been and still is preeminently Dōgen's Zen.

The history of Japanese Rinzai Zen is quite different. During a period of one hundred and seventy-five years after the return of Eisai from China, twenty lines of Rinzai Zen teaching were brought to Japan and established there either by Chinese masters, many of them fleeing the disturbed political conditions in China, or by Japanese monks who had gone to China to study with Chinese masters and had received the Seal of Transmission from them. One of the more notable of the Japanese pilgrim monks was Shinchi Kakushin 心地覺心 (1207–1298), who studied under Wu-mên Hui-k'ai 無門慧開 (Mumon Ekai, 1183–1260). Kakushin returned to Japan in 1254, bringing with him his master's famous koan collection *Wu-mên-kuan* (*Mumonkan*). Another pilgrim monk was Nampo Jōmyō 南浦紹明 (1235–1309), better known by his Imperially bestowed title Daiō Kokushi 大應國師. He went to China in 1259 and took his training under the Chinese Lin-chi master Hsüt'ang Chih-yü 虛堂智愚 (Kidō Chigu, 1185–1269), returning to Kyoto in 1267. The last of the Rinzai teaching lines was that founded by the Japanese monk Daisetsu Sonō 大拙祖能 (1313–1377), who left for China in 1344 and returned in 1358. Thereafter, while the intercourse between Chinese and Japanese Zen did not cease, it gradually diminished. No outstanding master appeared and no new teaching line was established for another three hundred years.

The Kamakura period (1185–1333) saw the rapid rise to prominence of Japanese Rinzai Zen. Great headquarter temples were erected at Kamakura and Kyoto, and branch temples established throughout the country under the aegis of emperors, shoguns, and feudal lords. This illustrious patronage, to which was added that of artists, intellectuals, warriors, and wealthy merchants, continued on through the Ashikaga period (1338–1573). During this period Rinzai temples became the centers of inspiration for an aesthetic flowering that has, correctly or incorrectly, made Zen and Japanese culture almost synonymous words. Rinzai Zen, now completely adapted to its new environment, settled down into comfortable complacency. All the Chinese and Japanese monks who had brought Rinzai Zen to Japan could trace their lineage directly back to the founder Lin-chi I-hsüan (Rinzai Gigen). All had brought with them the texts as well as the koans handed down to them by their teachers, and continued to use these in instructing their disciples. Whatever differences there may have been in their teaching were due to traditions in their teaching lines or to personal preferences, not to differences in basic principles.

The Japanese genius for the preservation of tradition fostered the continued transmission of the koans and their answers in the forms in which they had originally been handed down. Little attempt at innovation seems to have been made. Only a very few new koans were created by Japanese masters, and in their commentaries upon texts these masters followed closely the commentaries traditional in their own teaching lines. One thing should, perhaps, be mentioned here, however. The monks who came to Japan in the Kamakura period had brought with them, in addition to Zen texts, works on the Neo-Confucianism of Sung, and were the first to introduce these to Japan. With many Zen priests, the study of these Neo-Confucian texts became a new and added interest. Though it cannot be said that Japanese Rinzai Zen was influenced by Confucianism, a tinge of it can occasionally be discerned in the writings of later Rinzai Zen men.

We have little specific information about the way in which the Japanese masters instructed their students in koans during these centuries. On the whole, the manner of transmission was probably as traditional as were the koans transmitted. But one difference is apparent. While the Chinese masters may have earlier begun to instruct some of their disciples individually in their private rooms, the coming of Japanese students encouraged this practice. Few, if any, Japanese monks were acquainted with spoken Chinese when they first arrived in China, but all could write Chinese. From the first the Chinese masters apparently received their Japanese disciples individually in their rooms, and instructed them through an exchange of written questions and answers. When the Japanese monks returned home to become masters themselves, though there was no barrier of language between them and their disciples, they continued the practice of giving koan instruction in private, and this practice seems to have become generally accepted in Japan.

The stagnation into which Rinzai Zen had sunk by the beginning of the Tokugawa era (1603–1867) was disturbed in the middle of the 17th century by the arrival at Nagasaki in 1654 of Yin-yüan Lung-ch'i 隱元隆琦 (Ingen Ryūki, 1592–1673). Ingen, to give him the Japanese name by which he was later always known, came to Japan as a refugee from the Manchus. He was a master of the Lin-chi School, and had at one time resided at the Huang-po-shan 黃檗山 (Ōbakuzan) in Fukien Province. The Zen which Ingen brought with him was late Ming dynasty Zen with all its accretions. Neither the Rinzai nor Sōtō sects of Japanese Zen received Ingen with much cordiality. Eventually the reigning emperor granted him land at Uji, near Kyoto, where, with the help of craftsmen and artisans who had accompanied him from China, he built an imposing monastery and temple in late Ming style, which he named the Mampuku-ji 萬福寺 after the original temple at Huang-po-shan. The fresh ideas in art, architecture, literary studies, and monastic organization introduced by Ingen had a direct influence that was far reaching in many fields. The new teaching and teaching methods he brought with him, however, though they may have had some indirect influence on later Rinzai Zen, were openly adopted only within the walls of the temples of the Ōbaku Sect which he founded. Ingen's coming marked the beginning of the end of the long lethargy into which the world of Rinzai Zen had sunk. Less than fifty years later Hakuin Ekaku 白隱慧鶴 appeared and shook that world to its foundations.

SUGIYAMA Iwajirō 杉山岩次郎 was born January 19, 1686,

in the village of Hara, situated at the foot of Mount Fuji on the Tōkaidō, the main road between Edo (Tokyo) and the old capital Kyoto. The name Hakuin Ekaku, by which he has always been known, is a combination of his two religious names. The temple priest who shaved his head as a youth gave him the name Ekaku; he himself adopted the name Hakuin in his early thirties. The *gō* or literary name he took was Kokurin 鵠林. His father was a samurai and his mother the daughter of the owner of a post station in the village.

As the youngest of five children, Hakuin was much with his mother, a devotee of the Nichiren 日蓮 Sect, and her religious nature had a deep influence upon him. He was a highly sensitive boy and gifted with a remarkable memory. At four he is said to have known by heart over three hundred of the local songs. When he was eight years old, after attending a service at which a section of the *Lotus Sutra* was chanted, he returned home and recited it exactly as he had heard it. At another time, a sermon on the Eight Hot Hells so stimulated the child's naturally excitable imagination that for a long time he lived in constant fear of experiencing their torments.

At the age of fifteen he gained his parents' consent to become a monk at the Shōin-ji 松蔭寺, a small Zen temple in his native village. Not long afterwards the temple priest became ill, and Hakuin went to live at the monastery of Daishō-ji 大聖寺 in the nearby town of Numazu. There he continued his training for several years. In 1705, when he was nineteen, he went through a mental crisis which plunged him into deep despair and led him to set out on a pilgrimage that took him from temple to temple in various parts of the country.

One fine summer day, the abbot of the Zuiun-ji 瑞雲寺, a temple in present Gifu Prefecture where Hakuin was then staying, put his library containing books on Buddhism, Confucianism, and Taoism, out to air. Seeing them, Hakuin, who was still uncertain of the path he wished to pursue in life, determined to settle the matter by picking up one of the volumes at random and letting it decide his fate. The book he chose chanced to be a famous collection of anecdotes from the lives of the old Chinese Zen masters. When he read in it the story of how Shih-shuang Ch'u-yüan 石霜楚圓 (Sekisō Soen, 986–1039) kept himself awake during his long meditation vigils by sticking himself in the thigh with a gimlet, young Hakuin resolved to continue his training until he, too, had attained enlightenment.

Hakuin then set out again on his pilgrimage. In 1708 he settled down for a time at the Eigan-ji 英巖寺 in Niigata Prefecture and devoted himself to zazen and koan study. Early one morning, after a night spent in meditation, he had his first glimpse of satori. For him the experience was so overwhelming that he was certain no one in hundreds of years had had so deep a satori as he. When the master of Eigan-ji refused to approve his enlightenment, Hakuin visited a number of other masters, hoping to get their recognition. No one agreed with him. Finally, his pride decidedly humbled, he came to Dōkyō Etan 道鏡慧端 (1642–1721) of the Shōju-an 正受庵 in Nagano Prefecture. This stern master subjected Hakuin to the hardest possible discipline, and, though he stayed with Etan only eight months—he was recalled to Numazu by the illness of his former teacher at the Daishō-ji—Hakuin succeeded in attaining his first real satori and his master's acknowledgment of it. Hakuin had previously had a number of teachers and later was to have others as well, but Shōju Rōjin 正受老人, as Etan was popularly known, was his real master. Throughout his entire life Hakuin never ceased being grateful to the old man.

In 1710 Hakuin was back in the Shōin-ji, the little temple in Hara where he had first been a novice. That same year, as the result of the strenuous practices he had subjected himself to, he had a severe nervous breakdown. After consulting several medical men and receiving no help from them, he finally sought out Hakuyūshi 白幽子, a hermit living in the mountains northeast of Kyoto. Through certain curious methods taught him by Hakuyūshi, Hakuin was able to cure himself completely.

Hakuin gave his first sermon two years later at the Shōin-ji. He was then twenty-six. But he soon resumed his wanderings, studying koans with various masters in different parts of the country. His satori experiences increased in frequency and depth. The death of his father in 1716—his mother had died some years earlier—again brought him back to Hara and the Shōin-ji. There he began to preach and teach. In 1718 he went to Kyoto and resided for a short time at the headquarters temple of Myōshin-ji 妙心寺. Upon his return to Hara he settled down in the Shōin-ji, never again to leave it for long.

Hakuin's fame now began to spread through the country, and disciples and lay followers came to him in ever increasing numbers. For the rest of his long life he taught and lectured continuously. Over the years he discoursed and commentated upon all the important Zen koan collections, many of the works of the Chinese Zen masters, and a few of the Buddhist sutras. He was a voluminous writer. His writings on Zen, for the most part in Chinese style, are rough, vigorous, and full of vivid imagery and picturesque expressions. For his lay followers, many of them the simple people of the neighboring farms and villages, he wrote in Japanese, using the Japanese syllabary which they could easily read. These writings, in which above all he stressed morality, obedience, and a virtuous life, were often punctuated with charming songs and verses of his own making.

Hakuin trained his disciples severely in traditional methods, exhorting them to zazen practice and further and further study of koans. His own experience of koan study under many different masters had given him a familiarity with the koans and the methods then in use in different teaching lines. He systematized these koans and methods to some extent himself, and this systematization was completed later by the most able of his many heirs. Furthermore, he created a considerable number of new koans, the most famous of which is that known as "The Sound of the Single Hand."

Hakuin's own deep and repeated satori experiences led him to encourage his students to strive for the same profound penetration as he had attained. Like his great Chinese predecessor Ta-hui, he insisted upon satori above everything else. But unlike Ta-hui, who had urged deeper and deeper satori through the continuously deeper introspection of a koan or koans but had made no attempt at any systematization of study, Hakuin considered that, after satori had once really been experienced, this satori should be gradually deepened and deepened by means of a systematized after-satori training. He divided Zen training into two parts: satori, and training after satori. The system originated by him and completed by his disciples is explained in detail by Isshū Rōshi in PART Two of this book.

But teaching, lecturing, and writing exhausted neither Hakuin's talents nor his tremendous energy. He encouraged and supervised the reprinting of the *Hannya shingyō* and the *Kannon gyō* 觀音經. He restored at least one temple in addition to his own Shōin-ji, and was instrumental in the rebuilding of two more, one of them the beautiful mountain monastery of Ryūtaku-ji 龍澤寺 in nearby Mishima, where he installed his great disciple Tōrei Enji 東嶺圓慈 (1721–1792). Moreover, Hakuin was a brilliant painter and calligrapher in the true Zen style. A thousand or more examples of his work have come down to us, and his genius in this field is only now being fully recognized. He is also said to have carved the wooden statue of himself in the possession of the Shōin-ji, a statue that shows him in full robes, grasping a long and menacing stick, eyes sharply penetrating, and the whole figure alive with restrained power. If this was the master his disciples faced in their koan interviews with him, their hearts must indeed have quailed and cold sweat run down their bodies.

But Hakuin had a warm and human side as well. Due to his own "meditation illness" in his youth, he showed much concern for the health of his disciples and often instructed them in the practices he had learned from the old hermit Hakuyūshi. Also, Hakuin was much beloved by the more humble among his lay followers. They came to him constantly for advice on the problems facing them in their daily life, a life which at that time was particularly bitter for the peasantry. Hakuin's kindness and helpfulness never failed. In his religious instruction to them he was always broad-minded, often recommending the teachings and practices of other schools of Buddhism when he felt that these answered their simple needs better than the austere practices of Rinzai Zen. Where his Zen students were concerned, however, Hakuin was opposed to any way but that of the traditional Rinzai School. He often spoke out harshly against the "silent-illumination" meditation of the Sōtō Sect and the *nembutsu* practice followed by adherents of the Pure Land sects.

Hakuin's teaching to his own disciples and to all Zen students may be summed up simply in this way: Men must realize Absolute Mind through their zazen practice and their koan study; through continued zazen practice, koan study, and daily life that realization must be ever deepened so that it may be made visible in every thought, word, and act, whatsoever these may be. Morality is the foundation stone of practice; without morality there can be no true practice and therefore no true attainment. And, finally, health of body must be preserved in order to carry the practice on to its completion.

Hakuin Ekaku died quietly in his sleep at the Shōin-ji, January 18, 1769, at the age of eighty-three.

And now the whole world of Japanese Rinzai Zen began to awake. Monks' Halls or *sōdō* 僧堂 were gradually established in connection with those headquarter temples that did not already have them, and at some of the sub-temples as well. The masters or *rōshi* 老師 in charge of these sodos were all Hakuin's disciples—he is said to have had ninety odd—or their direct heirs. Changes were made in the arrangement of the meditation halls and the monks' living quarters, some of these following the style Ingen had earlier introduced at the Mampuku-ji. All aspects of daily life were strictly regulated, and a curriculum of study instituted that consisted of zazen, koan study, daily labor, begging, and sutra chanting. The year was divided into spring and autumn terms of three months each when the monks lived and studied in the sodo; each term was followed by a vacation period of three months during which the monks were free to return to their home temples in other parts of the country.

The system of koan instruction originated by Hakuin now replaced all previous methods of instruction. This system was developed and refined by his disciples, including his direct heir Gasan Jitō 峨山慈棹 (1727-1797). But it was Gasan's two heirs, Inzan Ien 隱山惟琰 (1751-1814) and Takujū Kosen 卓洲胡遷 (1760-1833), who finally fixed "Hakuin Zen" in the two teaching styles current today. Neither Hakuin nor his disciples compiled any collections of koans, at least none that were ever published. (The koans that Hakuin created are still transmitted only by word of mouth to the student in the master's room.) Except for Hakuin's koans, generally given in the earlier stages of koan study, the masters took their koans from the old Chinese collections, *Wu-mên-kuan (Mumonkan)*, *Pi-yen lu (Hekigan roku)*, *Lin-chi lu (Rinzai roku)*, and *Hsü-t'ang lu tai-pieh (Kidō roku daibetsu)*, and from a collection made in Japan shortly before Hakuin's time known as *Kattō shū*. In the Inzan and Takujū lines, the answers to the koans were more or less standardized for each line respectively.

Another innovation that seems to have been instituted either by Hakuin or his disciples was the use of *jakugo* 著語 or "capping phrases" in koan study. Long before, Fên-yang Shan-chao had appended his own verses, epitomizing the import of the koan in poetical language, to each of the hundred koans that comprised one of his collections, and Zen men had been writing such verses on koans ever since. Now, when the student had satisfied the master as to his understanding of a koan, he was asked to bring to the master a line or two in verse or prose which, as with Fên-yang's verses, summarized the import of the koan. In this case, however, the capping phrase was not to be original with the student; it was to be a quotation taken from the literature, preferably secular, of any period. *Zenrin kushū*, an anthology of quotations from Chinese and Japanese sources compiled shortly before Hakuin's time, with which he is said to have become acquainted in his youth, was the principal source for these jakugo. A detailed description of this anthology constitutes PART THREE of this work. Masters of the Inzan line used jakugo for most, but not all, of the koans; those of the Takujū School used jakugo for all koans, often demanding several successively for a single koan. As with the answers to the koans, the jakugo for each koan seems to have been more or less standardized in each of these two teaching lines.

In the curriculum of the monastery, koan study unquestionably held first place. Every monk studied koans under the personal supervision of the master of the monastery. When a monk entered the sodo the master gave him his first koan; he did not choose it himself, as would seem to have been the general custom previously. On this koan the monk meditated until he had attained a satori deep enough to satisfy the master that he was ready to begin his "practice after satori." The attainment of the first satori, or *kenshō* 見性, was expected to take two or three years, the full training after satori, from ten to fifteen years more.

The master or roshi met his student-monks individually at stated times for a private interview called *sanzen* 参禪. This might take place several times a day during the weeks especially devoted to meditation and known as *sesshin* 接(攝)心, or only once or twice a day at other times. The etiquette for such an interview was definitely prescribed and extremely formal. The monk entered the master's room after a series of deep bows outside and inside the entrance to it, sat down facing the master, stated his koan immediately, and gave the answer he had arrived at. If the master was convinced that the student's insight tallied with the koan, he might accept the answer, then ask him to bring a jakugo for it at the next regular time for sanzen. If not, the master might give the student a word of encouragement or drop a hint to let him know that he was on the wrong path. Most often, however, the master did not utter a single word; he merely rang a little bell at his right hand, indicating that the interview was over and he was ready to receive the next student. Etiquette demanded that the monk leave the room at once after making the usual bows. Thus there was little or no opportunity for the student to ask a question or even to open his mouth after his first words.

On certain fixed days the roshi gave a *teishō* 提唱, or lecture, to the monks. For this lecture he took a high seat facing the altar in the center of the main hall of the monastery, and discoursed, in the fashion set by Hakuin, on one of the old koan collections, taking up one "case" or a part of a case at each lecture successively until he had covered the entire collection.

Such is the manner of koan study that has prevailed in Japanese Rinzai Zen from the time of Hakuin and his disciples to the present day. Many of the forms and ceremonies still observed in Zen temple life can be traced back to customs current in China during the Sung and Yüan dynasties and in Japan during the Kamakura and Ashikaga periods. Certain definitely feudalistic elements are discernible in the method of koan instruction which Hakuin originated. The period in which he lived was the middle of the Tokugawa era, an era when all aspects of Japanese life were frozen in a rigid feudalistic pattern. It is only natural, therefore, that the changes Hakuin made, revolutionary though many of them must have seemed in his own day, should have conformed, in externals at least, to the period of history in which he lived. And the Japanese reverence for tradition where form is concerned has preserved these externals punctiliously.

The upsurge of vitality in Rinzai Zen to which Hakuin gave the impetus was dealt a heavy blow in the first years of the Meiji era (1868-1912), when the government withdrew its support from all Buddhist temples and monasteries, deprived many of them of their holdings in land, and for a short time even openly persecuted them. But before many years had passed, despite the government's continued official support of Shintō, the various Buddhist sects, including those of Rinzai and Sōtō Zen, regained much of their earlier vigor. In the Rinzai monasteries of Kamakura and Kyoto several powerful

Rinzai masters appeared who attracted to themselves talented disciples and lay adherents of importance in governmental, educational, and financial circles.

The strong spirit of nationalism which, fostered by the government, began to take root in Japan in the last years of the 19th century, was accompanied by a mounting national pride in the great periods of the country's history. The stern martial code of the samurai of the Kamakura era was glorified and held up as the ideal way of conduct for citizen and soldier alike; the artistic creations of the Ashikaga era were reappraised and introduced to the western world as a flowering in the field of the arts that could only have been produced by the Japanese genius. Japanese Zen was credited with having been the source of those unique spiritual qualities with which the best in Japanese culture was now seen to be infused. The use of religion as a legitimate political expedient had been accepted throughout Japanese history, and it was accepted again. The military faction, fast rising to absolute power, saw in certain Zen practices a possible tool for the accomplishment of their ends. They now openly solicited assistance from Rinzai Zen in stimulating and sustaining the people's ardor. They were not refused.

The end of the last war found Rinzai Zen in a state of spiritual and physical exhaustion. The new land redistribution laws took away from the temples all but the last of their acres, and, with supporters reduced to the few who were still faithful believers, the priests in many cases were forced to find outside employment in order to keep their temple roofs in repair and themselves in daily necessities. The attention of the nation was completely concentrated on reconstruction and the regaining of material prosperity.

The Japanese Zen masters of today are trying faithfully to carry on their teaching against tremendous odds. Furthermore, they are bound by a traditional system which, as regards many of its forms, is a relic of the feudal age. All are aware of this, but the great problem facing them is how to adapt to modern life and thought without losing the very essence of

Zen itself. The West's, to them, unanticipated interest in Zen and the slightly reviving interest of Japanese laymen may help to point a way. Zen has always made the same teaching available to laymen as to monks. The masters who have transmitted traditional Zen have, with few exceptions, always been temple men, but from the earliest times laymen have been among their more distinguished disciples.

Enlightenment, the personal experience of Reality, is man's ultimate experience. The quest for this experience is the most difficult quest upon which he can embark. It demands of him faith, determination, sacrifice, and, above all, passion. Without the sustained sense of urgency which passion imparts, the goal cannot be achieved. All the great men of Zen have understood this. The koans were in part devised to keep the sense of urgency sustained during the intervals when the heat of passion subsided. The seemingly unsolvable problem goads the disciple on mercilessly; when at last it is solved, the assurance that the insight attained tallies with the insight of enlightened men before him renews the disciple's faith in himself and his determination to press on. The koans are indeed peerless aids in the quest for the experience of enlightenment.

PART TWO

KOAN STUDY IN RINZAI ZEN

I. THE FOUR VOWS

ZEN is "without words, without explanations, without instruction, without knowledge." Zen is self-awakening only. Yet if we want to communicate something about it to others, we are forced to fall back upon words.

I am only a practicing Zen monk. I have no scholarly learning and no literary accomplishments. However, using my own experience as the basis, in the following pages I shall try to tell you something about the course of study and practice followed by Zen monks during the years they spend in the training hall.

But first I should like to introduce you to the Four Vows. Every Buddhist not only recites the Four Vows morning and evening, but tries to keep them always in mind and to carry them out to the best of his ability throughout the course of his entire lifetime. For Zen monks, especially, these are the most important of all vows:

> Sentient beings are numberless;
> I take a vow to save them.
> The deluding passions are inexhaustible;
> I take a vow to destroy them.
> The Gates of Dharma are manifold;
> I take a vow to enter them.
> The Buddha-way is supreme;
> I take a vow to complete it.

This is *the* Vow. Various karmic relations played a part in my going to New York in the spring of 1955 to give the talks on which this book is based, but this Vow was the fundamental cause. If you will firmly establish the Four Vows in your heart, my purpose will be more than fulfilled.

II. SEEING INTO ONE'S OWN NATURE (1)

WHEN we Zen students enter the zendo, needless to say our first aim is to attain the state of *kenshō*, that is, "to attain insight into our own real nature." If you ask me the question, "What is kensho—what is this 'seeing into one's own real nature'?" I am afraid I can give you no other answer than to say : "Kensho is just kensho, nothing more."

Our great masters of olden times have described the experience in various ways. One master said that kensho is just like coming back to life again after having lost your hold on the edge of a precipice and fallen to your death. Another master has said that kensho is the moment when you die the Great Death. And another has spoken of it as the state in which Great Life clearly manifests itself.

Though there are many ways of describing this state of seeing into one's own nature, all are merely something our old masters have said *about* it. The actual experience of true kensho can be attained only by yourself through your own self-awaken-

37

ing in your own body. There is no other way. In order to reach this state of seeing into our own nature, we Zen monks labor diligently and painstakingly day and night. A Zen monk without kensho is not worth a penny.

The experience of kensho has been handed down directly from Shakyamuni Buddha through successive generations of patriarchs to men of the present by means of the " transmission of Mind by mind." As long as the direct experience of kensho continues to be thus transmitted from generation to generation, Zen will not disappear, regardless of whether great temples and religious establishments exist or not.

Daitō Kokushi, founder of the Daitoku-ji, in his last admonition spoke emphatically about the importance of kensho for Zen monks. His words are something like this:

" Some of you may preside over large and flourishing temples with Buddha-shrines and rolls of scripture gorgeously decorated with gold and silver, you may recite the sutras, practice meditation, and even lead your daily lives in strict accordance with the precepts, but if you carry on these activities without having the eye of kensho, every one of you belongs to the tribe of evil spirits.

" On the other hand, if you carry on your activities with the eye of kensho, though you pass your days living in a solitary hut in the wilderness, wear a tattered robe, and eat only boiled roots, you are the man who meets me face to face every day and requites my kindness."

Seeing into our own real nature is the first principle for Zen monks. Therefore, always keeping foremost in our minds the koan we have been given, we never cease seeking kensho day and night, night and day. In order that you may know with what seriousness we seek it, I shall tell you about Eka Daishi, the second patriarch of our Zen Sect in China. This will afford a better example than anything I could tell you from my own experience.

Long ago Bodhidharma was staying at a small temple called Shōrin-ji, practicing the zazen we call wall-gazing. At that time there was a lofty-minded man, Jinkō by name, who had lived a long time near the I and Lo rivers in Honan. He had read widely and deeply. He paid no attention to gaining a livelihood, but loved to roam among the lakes and mountains. He used to say: " Alas, the teachings of Confucius and Lao-tzu are concerned only with propriety and conduct; the *Chuang-tzu* and the *Book of Changes* fall far short of exhausting the Marvelous Principle."

One day he said to himself : " I have heard that Bodhidharma, the Great Teacher, is now living at the Shōrin-ji. The sage is not far away; I must go to that mysterious place."

So he went to the Shōrin-ji. But, since the Master constantly sat erect and silent facing the wall, Jinkō heard from him no words of instruction or encouragement. Then Jinkō thought to himself: "In their search for Tao, the men of olden times crushed their bones and took out the marrow, or cut their veins and drained their blood to appease the hunger of others; they spread their hair upon the muddy road for a buddha to walk upon; they threw themselves from the top of a cliff to feed the starving tigers below. The men of olden times did this. Am I not also a man ? "

On the ninth night of the twelfth month there was a violent storm of wind and snow, and the cold pierced to the bone. Jinkō stood motionless through it all. When dawn broke, the snow reached above his waist. Seeing this, the Master was filled with pity. " You have been standing in the snow for a long time," he said. " What do you seek ?"

With his voice choked with tears, Jinkō replied : " My only request is that the Master, in his mercy, may deign to open the Gate of Sweet Dew and save all sentient beings."

" The incomparable Marvelous Tao of all the Buddhas," replied the Master, "is attained only by long diligence in a practice difficult to practice, and by long endurance of that which it is difficult to endure. Why should you, with your shallow mind and arrogant heart, beg me for the True Vehicle and suffer such hardships in vain ?"

Upon hearing these words, Jinkō drew his sword from under his robe, cut off his left arm at the elbow, and placed it before the Master. At this, the Master knew Jinkō to be a vessel of Dharma. He said : " All the Buddhas, when they seek Tao, forget their bodies for the sake of Dharma. You have cut off your arm. Now you, also, are capable of seeking."

" May I hear from you about the Dharma Seal of All the Buddhas ? " Jinkō asked.

" The Dharma Seal of All the Buddhas is not obtained from another," the Master said.

" Your disciple's mind is as yet without repose," said Jinkō. " I beg you, Master, let me have repose of mind."

" Bring me your mind and I will repose it for you," the Master replied.

" Though I seek for my mind, I cannot get it," said Jinkō.

" I have reposed your mind for you," said the Master.

At these words Jinkō attained satori.

In such ways as this our patriarchs strove at the risk of their lives to attain kensho—to attain insight into their own real nature. If it was for the sake of Dharma, they did not hesitate to sacrifice their bodies or lay down their lives. Following their example, we also sit and practice meditation. Of course we do not go to the extreme of cutting off our arms. If we were to imitate Jinkō, however many arms we might have they would not suffice. Nevertheless we do such things as practicing zazen stark naked in mid-winter.

Nanshinken, the late Rōshi of the Nanzen-ji Sodo, in his day had the reputation of being the most severe of all the sodo roshis in Japan. Whenever he found any of us negligent in our practice, he would wield his *nyoi* ruthlessly, and, every O Sesshin, many of us would bear the resultant bumps on our heads. I am still deeply grateful for Nanshinken's nyoi.

I am told that a pearl is produced only through the pearl-oyster's enduring the pain of having a grain of sand bore into its flesh, fighting against it, and protecting itself against it. We, also, by fighting all kinds of difficulties and overcoming them, strive to develop the jewel of spiritual cultivation.

III. SEEING INTO ONE'S OWN NATURE (2)

BECAUSE the experience of kensho—seeing into one's own real nature—is the pivot of Zen, and because the attainment of this experience is the fundamental aim of our Zen practice, our patriarchs have spoken and written many stimulating and encouraging words in order to urge their students on to more strenuous efforts. The great Japanese Zen Master Hakuin is one of those who have much to say on kensho, and in his *Sokkō roku kaien fusetsu* explains kindly and with scrupulous care the preparatory attitude of mind necessary for this experience. He says:

If you wish to seek Buddha, you must first have insight into your own real nature. Without this insight, what benefit will you derive from reciting the Nembutsu or chanting the sutras? The word "Buddha" means "Awakened." When you awaken, it is your own mind that is Buddha. If somewhere else than in your own mind you seek a Buddha having a tangible form, you are a foolish fellow. It is like a man who is seeking for fish. He must first of all look in the water because, since fish are the product of water, outside water there are no fish. Just so, he who wishes to seek Buddha must first of all look into his own mind because, since Buddha is the product of mind, outside mind there is no Buddha.

You may ask: "If, as you say, there is no Buddha outside mind, how can one awaken one's own mind and get to the bottom of it?"

I reply: "Is it mind that asks this question? Is it nature? Do you call it spirit, or do you call it soul? Does it reside on the inside, on the outside, or in the middle? Is it blue or yellow, red or white? You yourself must examine closely. When you are standing, examine closely; when you are sitting, examine closely. While you are eating your rice, while you are drinking your tea, while you are speaking, while you are silent, carry on this investigation intently and earnestly. Under no circumstances search among the teachings of the sutras or in written words. Never ask your teachers to explain. But when your activity of mind is exhausted and your capacity for feeling comes to a dead end, if something should take place not unlike the cat springing upon the mouse or the mother hen hatching her eggs, then in a flash great livingness surges up. This is the moment when the phoenix escapes from the golden net, when the crane breaks the bars of its cage. But, though you spend twenty or thirty years of your life in fruitless effort, and even up to the moment of death fail to break through, you must vow never even for a moment to think that the tales of any decrepit old man or woman can be of benefit to you in any way. If you do, their words will cling to your bones and stick to your skin, and you will never be able to rid yourself of them, to say nothing of achieving the ultimate aim of the patriarchs.

That is why a man of old said: "For the study of Zen there are three essential requirements." What are these three essential requirements? The first is a great root of faith; the second is a great ball of doubt; the third is great tenacity of purpose. A man who lacks any one of these is like a three-legged kettle with one broken leg.

What is a root of faith? It is nothing less than the belief that every man possesses his own intrinsic nature into which he can attain insight, and that there is a Fundamental Principle which can be completely penetrated. Just this. But, even though he has sincere faith, if a man does not bring concentrated doubt to bear upon the koans that are difficult to pass through, he cannot get to the bottom of them and penetrate them completely. And, though this ball of doubt be firmly solidified, if it is not succeeded by great tenacity of purpose, it will not be shattered. Therefore it is said that, for slothful sentient beings, Nirvana endures for three asamkhyeya kalpas, for intrepid sentient beings, the attainment of Buddhahood takes place in an instant of thought. You must always be ardent.

The study of Zen is like boring wood to get fire. The wisest course is to forge straight ahead without stopping. If you rest at the first sign of heat, and then again as soon as the first wisp of smoke arises, even though you bore for three asamkhyeya kalpas, you will never see a spark of fire. My native place is close to the seashore, barely a few hundred paces from the beach. Suppose a man of my village is concerned because he does not know the flavor of sea water, and wants to go and taste it for himself. If he turns back after having taken only a few steps, or even if he returns after having taken a hundred steps, in either case when will he ever know the ocean's bitter salty taste? But, though a man comes from as far as the mountains of Koshu or Shinshu, Hida or Mino, if he goes straight ahead without stopping, within a few days he will reach the shore, and, the moment he dips the tip of one finger into the sea and licks it, he will instantly know the taste of the waters of the distant oceans and the nearby seas, of the southern beaches and the northern shores, in fact of all the sea water in the world.

Thus Hakuin Zenji painstakingly explains the matter for the sake of those of us who are studying Zen. Although he tells us not to search in the sutras and other writings, not to be led astray by the words of men, this is very difficult indeed. However, our patriarchs have not left us without assistance. I said previously that, in our ceaseless seeking for kensho, we Zen monks always keep foremost in our minds the koan we have been given. What is the koan we are given when we first enter the monastery and begin our Zen study? Our teacher usually selects one of these three:

The Sixth Patriarch asked the head monk Myō: "Thinking neither of good nor of evil, at this very moment what was your original aspect before your father and mother were born?"

A monk asked Master Jōshū: "Has the dog Buddha-nature or not?" Jōshū answered: "Mu!"

Hakuin Zenji used to say to his disciples: "Listen to the sound of the Single Hand!"

In the first line of his *Zazen wasan*, Hakuin Zenji says: "Sentient beings are intrinsically Buddha." When Shakyamuni was sitting under the Bodhi Tree and, on catching a glimpse of the morning star, came to his Great Awakening, he also exclaimed: "How wonderful! Every sentient creature is endowed with the intrinsic wisdom and virtuous characteristics of Tathāgata."

All the phenomena that are unfolding before our eyes, all, without any exception, just as they are, are the reality we see when we attain insight into our own real nature. All are Tathāgata. All sounds are the profound and exquisitely subtle voice of Dharma. Why is it impossible for us to receive them as they are? Shakyamuni Buddha, Hakuin, and all the patriarchs of the past have proclaimed: "Sentient beings are intrinsically Buddha," or, "Every sentient creature is endowed with the intrinsic wisdom and virtuous characteristics of Tathāgata." But though these sounds are correctly broadcasted, our receiving instruments emit only a confusion of noise, and, constantly engrossed in things as we are, we cannot distinguish the precious and subtle sounds lost in the interference. To say this does not mean that our receiving instruments are inferior. Such is not at all the case. Each one of us has exactly the same remarkable receiving instrument as the Buddha had. What is essential is to know how to adjust it.

When we enter the sodo, the first instruction we receive is, "Give up your life!" It is easy to pronounce the words "Give up your life!" but to do so is a difficult matter. However, if we do not put an end once and for all to that which is called "self" by cutting it off and throwing it away, we can never accomplish our practice. When we do, a strange world reveals itself to us, a world surpassing our reckoning, where he who has cast away his self gains everything, and he who grasps for everything with his illusory concepts in the end loses everything, even himself.

Of course, what I have been saying all this while is just a part of the confusion of sounds of which the world is so full. But I hope that every one of you, with your wonderful receiving instruments, may correctly catch the exquisite voice of Dharma and attain Shakyamuni's so-called "True Dharma Eye," "Marvelous Mind of Nirvana," and "True Form of the Formless." Whenever the din becomes unbearable, I beg you to practice zazen. Zazen is the peerless method of adjusting our receiving instruments.

IV. THE *HOSSHIN* AND *KIKAN* KOANS

THOUGH I have already spoken at some length on the subject of kensho or seeing into one's own true nature, I shall say a little more about it. Since kensho is the foundation of Zen, however much we may think about it, we still do not know it, and, however many times we may speak about it, we can never speak too often.

Hakuin Zenji, in his *Sokkō roku kaien fusetsu*, which I have previously quoted, has this further to say:

> My humble advice to you distinguished persons who study the profound mystery of the Buddha-dharma is this: Your close examination of yourself must be as urgent as saving your own head were it ablaze; your efforts to penetrate into your own original nature must be as tireless as the pursuit of an indispensable thing; your attitude toward the verbal teachings of the buddhas and patriarchs must be as hostile as that toward a deadly enemy.

In Zen, he who does not bring strong doubt to bear upon the koans is a dissolute, knavish good-for-nothing. Therefore it is said: "Underlying great doubt there is great satori; where there is thorough questioning there will be a thoroughgoing experience of awakening."

Do not say: "Since my worldly duties are many and troublesome, I cannot spare time to solidify my doubt firmly," or, "Since my thoughts are always flying about in confusion, I lack the power to apply myself to genuine concentration on my koan."

Suppose that, among the dense crowds of people in the hurly-burly of the market place, a man accidentally loses two or three pieces of gold. You will never find anyone who, because the place is noisy and bustling or because he has dropped his pieces of gold in the dirt, will not turn back to look for them. He pushes any number of people about, stirs up a lot of dust, and, weeping copious tears, rushes around searching for his gold. If he doesn't get it back into his own two hands, he will never regain his peace of mind. Do you consider the priceless jewel worn in the hair, your own inherent marvelous Tao, of less value than two or three pieces of gold?

On hearing Hakuin Zenji's kind words of admonition, any person of resolute purpose will certainly have his mettle aroused. But for one who is without aspiration, of course they will be but the recitation of the Nembutsu in a horse's ear. Treasuring such words of admonition in our hearts, and bearing always in mind the conduct of the patriarchs in their daily activities, we face squarely to the koan we have been given, study it faithfully, and work wholeheartedly. We pass beyond time, are not swayed by all kinds of external circumstances, keep our inner mind calm and composed, and make this mind firm and hard as an iron wall. If this concentrated reflection is built up continuously over one year, two years, three years, insight into one's own true nature will inevitably take place.

The realm which is revealed to us once we see into our own

true nature is none other than that known in Sanskrit as the *Dharmakāya*, and, in Japanese, the *hosshin*. Since the Dharmakāya has been explained backward and forward in the works of the various schools that depend upon the scriptures and their commentaries, I shall not take it up from the scholastic point of view. In *Rinzai roku*, the Zen Master Rinzai speaks about the Dharmakāya this way: "The pure light in each instant of thought is the Dharmakāya Buddha within your own house."

With the aid of our first koan we attain our first glimpse into the undifferentiated realm of the Dharmakāya. To deepen our insight into this realm, to become acquainted intimately with this, our original home, and to make it our constant dwelling place, we study many koans known as Dharmakāya koans, or, in Japanese, *hosshin* koans. Let me give you a few examples:

A monk asked Kassan Oshō: "What is the Dharmakāya?" "The Dharmakāya is without form," Kassan replied.

A monk once said to Dairyō Oshō: "The physical body decomposes. What is the indestructible Dharmakāya?" Dairyō answered with this verse:
" Blooming mountain flowers
Are like golden brocade;
Brimming mountain waters
Are blue as indigo."

When Ummon was asked, "What is the pure Dharmakāya?" he replied: "The flowering hedge [surrounding the privy]."

To Jun Oshō's verse on the Dharmakāya was this:
When the cows of Eshū are well fed with grain,
The horses of Ekishū have full stomachs.

This is like saying that, when an American sneezes, an Englishman catches cold.

Fu Daishi composed the following verse on the Dharmakāya:

Empty-handed, yet holding a hoe;
Walking, yet riding a water buffalo.

If, on coming upon expressions such as these, you feel as if you were meeting a close relative face to face at a busy crossroad and recognizing him beyond a question of a doubt, then you can be said to understand the Dharmakāya. But, if you use common sense to conjecture about it, or run hither and thither trying to follow the words of others, you will never know the Dharmakāya. An old master has said: " There are many intelligent men, but few who have attained insight into their own real nature." Truly this one thing—seeing into one's own real nature—is the eternal eye of Zen.

———

But now that we have once achieved kensho, if we stop here and do not go forward another step, we cannot experience the patriarchs' marvelous realm of differentiation. To save ourselves from this misfortune, it is necessary to pass through many intricate koans having to do with differentiation. The Zen term for the complex interlockings of differentiation is *kikan*, and the koans that have been devised to aid us in successfully dealing with these interlockings are called *kikan* koans.

In the *Hekigan roku* there is a passage that reads:

Jade is tested by fire, gold is tested by a touchstone, a sword is tested by a hair, water is tested by a stick. In our school, one word or one phrase, one action or one state, one entrance or one departure, one " Hello!" or one " How are you!" is used to judge the depth of the student's understanding, to observe whether he is facing forward or facing backward. If he is a fellow with blood in his veins, he will immediately go off, shaking his sleeves behind him, and, though you shout after him, he will not come back.

With the help of the *kikan* koans we release ourselves from the bonds that hold us fast, get out of the sticky morass in which we are floundering, and return to the unfettered freedom of the open fields. Some people may say: " If I have gained insight into my real nature once, that is enough. Why should I go further and study many *kikan* koans?" The old masters lashed out at such persons, calling them "earthworms living in the mud of self-accredited enlightenment." "We awaken to Reality suddenly, and are perceiving phenomena right now." As we master the interlockings of differentiation one by one, and our understanding becomes clearer and clearer, Reality becomes increasingly distinct.

The following are some of the koans used to enable us to manipulate these interlockings freely:

Tosotsu Etsu Oshō devised three barriers as tests for his students :

1. You pull out the weeds and study the profound mystery only in order to see into your original nature. Where is your original nature at this moment ?

2. One who has realized his own original nature escapes from birth-and-death. When the light of your eyes falls to the ground, how will you escape ?

3. One who has escaped from birth-and-death knows whither he goes. When the Four Great Elements that compose your body separate, where will you go?

A monk asked Master Jōshū : " What is the meaning of Bodhidharma's coming from the West ?"
"The cypress tree in the garden," Jōshū replied.

Three times the National Teacher Chū called to his attendant, and three times the attendant answered him. The National Teacher said : " I always used to think that I was beholden to you, but all along it was really you who were beholden to me."

We must make our way through the mass of complex interlockings that comprise the realm of differentiation, and enter the inner sanctuary of the patriarchs. To accomplish this, we must train ourselves by concentrated reflection on our koans over and over again. Daie Oshō used to say to people: " I have experienced great satori eighteen times, and lost count of the number of small satoris I have had." If even the old masters had to train themselves thus, surely we haven't a moment to waste.

When the power of kensho—the power of seeing into our own true nature—is weak, we cannot alter the karma clinging to us from the past that hinders our attainment. If the wisdom that comprehends differentiation is not completely bright, we cannot benefit sentient beings. But to make this differentiation-wisdom bright is a difficult undertaking indeed.

V. THE *GONSEN* KOANS

I have spoken at some length about the Dharmakāya or *hosshin* koans and about the *kikan* koans.   The next type of koan we take up in our Zen study is that known as the *gonsen* koan. *Gonsen* means literally "the study and investigation of words." *Gonsen* koans are those words and phrases of the patriarchs that are difficult to understand.   Now that we have succeeded in entering the Dharmakāya (*hosshin*), and in making our way through the interlockings of differentiation (*kikan*), we must devote our efforts to penetrating into the innermost meaning of words and phrases.

We often hear it said: " In our sect (i.e. the Zen Sect) there are no written letters to be set down, no words and phrases to be made known, no delusions to be freed from, no enlightenment to be attained."   But, if we were to sit down right here in what an old master has called " the deep pit of emancipation," we should, after all, be violating the true meaning of the Buddha-dharma.   Hence, for us students of Zen, beneath a single phrase there exists life and there exists death, within a single response there lies release and there lies capture, upon a single expression rests the realm of the myriad transformations which it is impossible for any man to know, whosoever he may be. This is why we must know the many subtle meanings within a single word.

Ummon Zenji said: "Men of immeasurable greatness are tossed about in the ebb and flow of words." If you can penetrate directly into words and understand them thoroughly, everything, from vicious words to the inane disputations of the world, will be transformed into ghee of the finest flavor.

Hakuin Zenji put it thus: "Dancing and singing are the voice of the Dharma."

An old master has said: "In our sect there are no words or phrases; there is not a single thing to give to men." But for the very reason that there are no words and phrases, words and phrases are the more wonderful. Because the hidden valley is without partiality, it echoes the footsteps of whomsoever enters it. For the very reason that there is not a single thing, the ten thousand things are the more mysterious. Because the great bell is of itself soundless, when it is struck by the bell-beam it reverberates with a flood of sound. Penetrating into the Fundamental Principle and penetrating into the teachings on it are not different from this. The four propositions of logic are abandoned and the hundred negations wiped out. Then, in whatsoever way or however freely you may speak, you can instantly "cut off the tongue of every man on earth." But if, because you desire the emancipation of only your own one body, you do not pass through the *gonsen* koans, how are you going to save sentient beings?

In the *Laṅkāvatāra-sūtra* we find this passage: "To penetrate into the Fundamental Principle and not to penetrate into the teachings on it is like opening your eyes in the dark. To penetrate into the teachings and not into the Fundamental Principle is like shutting your eyes in the daylight. To penetrate into both the Fundamental Principle and the teachings on it is like opening your eyes in the clear light of day." Perhaps by now you have come to realize the importance of these *gonsen* koans, these koans that are concerned with the study and investigation of words.

Long ago Bodhidharma described his teaching as: "A special transmission outside the scriptures; not founded upon words and letters; by pointing directly to man's own mind, it lets him see into his own true nature and thus attain Buddhahood." Frequently, as the result of misunderstanding this statement, people do not read the scriptures and the writings of the patriarchs, or they consider verbal teachings to be of minor importance. That so many of our own sect have today abandoned these studies is a matter for regret. When a teaching outside the scriptures is clearly understood, the teaching within the scriptures should not interfere with it. If a teaching outside the scriptures does not admit the teaching within the scriptures, then it is not a true teaching. When the insight into both is clear, there is no prejudice against either.

To illumine one's mind with old learning at a bright window during the day and to deepen one's discernment of the Principle by meditation in the Monks' Hall during the night, this is, indeed, to illumine one's own nature with the teachings and to illumine the teachings with one's own nature. Inside and outside are one, this and that are transcended. It is just like two mirrors mutually reflecting one another with no shadow between them.

But, though written words and spoken phrases can be the source of emancipation, they can be the source of bondage as well. Depending upon the way they are used, they become the finest ghee or the most vicious poison.

Now let me show you a few of the koans through the study of which we attain insight into the mystery of words:

A monk once said to Fuketsu Oshō: "Speech and silence tend toward separation [from IT] or concealment [of IT]. How shall we proceed so as not to violate IT?"
Fuketsu replied with the following verse:
"I always remember Kōnan in the spring,

> The partridges crying and flowers spilling their
> fragrance.

A monk asked Nansen: "Is there a truth that has not
been preached to men?"

"There is," said Nansen.

"What is this truth?" asked the monk.

Nansen answered: "This is not mind, this is not Buddha,
this is not a thing."

A monk asked Master Jōshū: "What is Jōshū?"

"East gate, west gate, south gate, north gate," Jōshū replied.

One day Chōsha Oshō went for a ramble in the mountains.
On his return to the monastery, the head monk said to him:
"Oshō, where have you been?"

"I have come from a ramble in the mountains," Chōsha
replied.

"Where did you go, Oshō?" the head monk inquired.

"Going, I followed the fragrant grasses; returning, I pursued the falling blossoms," answered Chōsha.

"How very springlike the feeling!" exclaimed the head
monk.

"Still better is the dripping of autumn dew from the full-
blown lotus flowers," returned Chōsha.

Setchō's *jakugo* was: "I am grateful to you for your answer."

We also study Haryō Oshō's "Three Pivotal Words":

1. A monk asked Haryō Oshō, "What is the Daiba Sect?"
   "Filling a silver bowl with snow," Haryō replied.
2. "What is the Blown Hair Sword?"
   "The tip of each branch of coral supports the moon."
3. "What is Tao?"
   "A bright-eyed man falls into a well."

Commenting upon these three questions and answers, Ummon said: "At some anniversary of my death, if you recite these 'Three Pivotal Words,' that will suffice to requite my kindness."

Such is the high regard in which we hold a phrase. But let me warn you, and this is the important point, if you are caught in the entanglement of words, you will lose your freedom.

When Shakyamuni was about to enter Nirvana, Mañjuśrī addressed him, saying: "I entreat the World Honored One to turn the Wheel of Dharma for the last time."

The World Honored One upbraided Mañjuśrī, saying: "From the day I entered the Deer Garden until I came here to the bank of the Hiraṇyavatī River, I have never uttered a single word."

Is this turning the Wheel of Dharma or not? It is difficult indeed fully to exhaust the mystery of words.

VI. THE *NANTŌ* KOANS

THE next type of koan we study is that known as the *nantō* koan. *Nantō* means "difficult to pass through," so the *nantō* koans are the koans most difficult to pass through. Even though we have smashed the tub of black lacquer with the help of the *hosshin* koans, moved through the multifold interlockings of the *kikan* koans, and, through the study of many *gonsen* koans, completed our investigation of those words of the patriarchs that are difficult to understand, to our regret we find that the dwelling place of the patriarchs is still as far away as the distant horizon. When we look up at it, it seems higher and higher; when we enter it, it seems deeper and deeper. Even for the patriarchs what formidable difficulties there were! This is the place called *nantō*, the place difficult to pass through. Not until we have penetrated these *nantō* koans one by one can we be said to be true monks.

In his *Sokkō roku kaien fusetsu*, Hakuin Zenji says:

My advice to you eminent persons who study this profound teaching is this: You resolute men must dauntlessly display your spirit and attain insight into your real nature once. But, the moment your insight into your own nature has become perfectly clear, discard the insight you have attained, and settle these *nantō* koans. Then you will understand beyond the question of a doubt the words of the *Nirvana Sutra* when it says: "All the Buddhas and World Honored Ones see their Buddha-nature with their own eyes as clearly as they see the mango fruit lying in the palms of their hands."

Furthermore, you will penetrate into the patriarchs' final experience. Then, for the first time, grasping in your two hands the talons and teeth from the cave of Dharma and wearing the supernatural talisman that wrests life from death, you can enter the realms of the Buddhas and sport in the world of the Maras; you can pull out the nails and wrench out the wedges, spread the cloud of Great Compassion, practice the almsgiving of the Great Dharma, and abundantly benefit those who come to you from all directions; yet all the while you are only an old monk with two horizontal eyes and a perpendicular nose, who, having nothing further to do, enjoys the greatest ease.

This is what is called being a true descendant of the patriarchs and a man who requites the kindness he has received. Now you may pass your days in tranquillity, drinking tea when there is tea, eating rice when there is rice. If there is nothing further to do, that is all right; if there is something to do, that is all right. The patriarchs cannot lay their hands on you, and you can spend ten thousand ounces of gold.

Until a Zen monk has reached this point he cannot be at ease even when drinking a cup of tea.

Nanshinken, my former teacher, often used to speak about this in his talks to the monks. "The practice of Zen," he would say, "is just like making a fine sword. The raw iron must be heated until it becomes red hot; then it must be beaten into shape, then put in the fire again, then thrust into cold water, then beaten into shape again—tempered and polished over and over and over again to bring it to completion. Then you will have a truly fine sword. There will be nothing it touches that such a sword does not cut through. On the other hand, if the tempering is insufficient, the blade will be defective or blunt. It won't cut the head off even a turnip."

For this reason, the more satoris you have attained the more you must experience, the clearer your understanding becomes the more you must study.

As examples of these *nantō* koans, let me show you these:

When the Taifu RIKU Kō and Nansen were talking one day, RIKU Kō said: " The Dharma Master Jō has said: ' Heaven-and-Earth and I have one and the same source; the ten thousand things and I have one and the same body.' Is this not extraordinary ?"

Pointing to a flower in the garden, Nansen said to the Taifu: " When men of today look at this flower, it seems to them like a dream."

The poet Setchō wrote the following verse in commentary upon Nansen's remark:

Hearing, seeing, understanding, knowing—
Each of these is not separate.
For him, mountains and rivers
Do not appear in the mirror.
When the frosty heaven's moon has set
And midnight nears,
Whose shadow with mine
Will the clear pool reflect, cold ?

Goso Hōen Zenji said: " It is like a water buffalo's passing through a window-lattice. Its head, horns, and four hoofs have all passed through. Why can't its tail pass through ? "

And another koan known as Sozan's Memorial Tower:

Once, when the monk who was director of affairs in the monastery came to talk with Sozan Nin Zenji about the construction of the Master's memorial tower, the Zenji said: "How much money will you give the builder?"

"That rests with you, Oshō," the monk replied.

"Is it better to give the builder three cash, or better to give him two cash, or better to give him one cash?" asked Sozan. "However, if you can speak, build the tower for me yourself."

The monk was dumbfounded.

At that time Rasan was living in a hermitage on the Daiyu Peak. One day a monk who came to the mountain to see him recounted this conversation between Sozan and the director of affairs at the monastery.

"Has anyone been able to speak?" asked Rasan.

"As yet, no one," replied the monk.

"Then go back to Sozan," said Rasan, "and tell him this: if you give the the builder three cash, you won't get a memorial tower in your entire lifetime; if you give him two cash, you and he together will be a single hand; if you give him one cash, you will do him such injury that his eyebrows and hair will fall out."

The monk returned and gave the message to Sozan. The Zenji assumed a dignified manner and, gazing far off toward the Daiyu Peak, bowed and said: "I had thought there was no man who could speak, but on the Daiyu Peak is an old Buddha who emits dazzling shafts of light reaching even to this distance. Nonetheless, he is a lotus blooming in midwinter."

Upon hearing of Sozan's words, Rasan said: "By my speaking thus, the tail hairs of the tortoise have suddenly grown several feet longer."

Addressing the assembly at the end of the summer sojourn, Suigan said: "My brothers, since the beginning of the

summer I have done a lot of talking. Look, have I any
eyebrows left ?"
Hofuku said: " The robber has a coward's heart."
Chōkei said: " Growing !"
Ummon said: " *Kan* !"

And then there is the koan known as Enkan's Rhinoceros-
horn Fan :

One day Enkan Oshō called to his attendant and said:
" Fetch me my rhinoceros-horn fan."
" The fan has been broken," said the attendant.
" If the fan has been broken, then bring me the rhinoceros
itself," Enkan returned.
The attendant had no reply.
Setchō's verse on this reads:
The rhinoceros-horn fan
Has long been in use,
But when a question is asked,
No one knows in truth what it is.
The boundless fresh breeze
And the horn on the head,
Just as rain clouds that have passed,
Are difficult to pursue.

When you have succeeded in passing through these and many
other *nantō* koans without any hesitation and without any doubt
—these koans that are difficult to believe, difficult to explain,
difficult to enter into, difficult to penetrate—you will have made
an exhaustive study of the *jiji muge hokkai*, the Dharma-world
where each thing interpenetrates and harmonizes perfectly with
every other thing without any hindrance whatsover, the realm of
complete effortlessness.

VII. THE *GOI* KOANS

WE are now approaching the summit of our formal study of Zen. Though we have penetrated many koans, including those difficult to pass through, the patriarchs want us to make a still deeper study of the doctrines of our sect.   To that end they would have us take up the *Tōzan goi*, the " Five Ranks " devised by Tōzan Ryōkai Zenji.

The Five Ranks has sometimes been called the philosophy of Zen.   However, without the insight we have gained as the result of passing through many previous koans, we would not be prepared to grasp the profound meaning of the Five Ranks. Intellectual ability has no part in the comprehension of the wisdom of the patriarchs.   The study of the Five Ranks is more nearly like a severe and final examination, for he who undertakes this study will be called upon not only to review all that he has previously come to understand, but to clarify, correlate, and deepen still further the insight he has attained.   He will have to polish again each facet of his spiritual jewel, which he has cut so laboriously and painstakingly. But, in doing so, he will see for the first time the total inclusiveness, perfect symmetry, and matchless beauty to which it has been brought under the training devised by the old masters.

Hakuin Zenji has given a penetrating commentary upon the Five Ranks in his *Keisō dokuzui*. I shall let him speak in my place. Perhaps after reading his words you will understand why we value the *goi* koans so highly.

THE FIVE RANKS OF THE APPARENT AND THE REAL: The Orally Transmitted Secret Teachings of the [Monk] Who Lived on Mount Tō

We do not know by whom the *Jeweled-mirror Samādhi* was composed. From Sekitō Oshō, Yakusan Oshō, and Ungan Oshō, it was transmitted from master to master and handed down within the secret room. Never have [its teachings] been willingly disclosed until now. After it had been transmitted to Tōzan Oshō, he made clear the gradations of the Five Ranks within it, and composed a verse for each rank, in order to bring out the main principle of Buddhism. Surely the Five Ranks is a torch on the midnight road, a ferry-boat at the riverside when one has lost one's way!

But alas! The Zen gardens of recent times are desolate and barren. "Directly-pointing-to-the-ultimate" Zen is regarded as nothing but benightedness and foolishness; and that supreme treasure of the Mahayana, the *Jeweled-mirror Samādhi's* Five Ranks of the Apparent and the Real, is considered to be only the old and broken vessel of an antiquated house. No one pays any attention to it.

[Today's students] are like blind men who have thrown away their staffs, calling them useless baggage. Of themselves they stumble and fall into the mud of heterodox views and cannot get out until death overtakes them. They never know that the Five Ranks is the ship that carries them across the poisonous sea surrounding the rank of the Real, the precious wheel that demolishes the impregnable prison-house of the two voids. They do not know the important road of progressive practice; they are not versed in the secret meaning within this teaching. Therefore they sink into the stagnant water of śrāvaka-hood or pratyeka-buddhahood. They fall into the black pit of withered sprouts and decayed seeds. Even the hand of Buddha would find it difficult to save them.

That into which I was initiated forty years ago in the room of Shōju I shall now dispense as the alms-giving of Dharma. When I find a superior person who is studying the true and profound teaching and has experienced the Great Death, I shall give this secret transmission to him, since it was not designed for men of medium and lesser ability. Take heed and do not treat it lightly!

How vast is the expanse of the sea of the doctrine, how manifold are the gates of the teaching! Among these, to be sure, are a number of doctrines and orally transmitted secret teachings, yet never have I seen anything to equal the perversion of the Five Ranks, the carping criticism, the tortuous explanations, the adding of branch to branch, the piling up of entanglement upon entanglement. The truth is that the teachers who are guilty of this do not know for what principle the Five Ranks was instituted. Hence they confuse and bewilder their students to the point that even a Śāriputra or an Ānanda would find it difficult to judge correctly.

Or, could it be that our patriarchs delivered themselves of these absurdities in order to harass their posterity unnecessarily? For a long time I wondered about this. But, when I came to enter the room of Shōju, the rhinoceros of my previous doubt suddenly fell down dead... Do not look with suspicion upon the Five Ranks, saying that it is not the directly transmitted oral teaching of the Tōzan line. You should know that it was only after he had completed his investigation of *Tōzan's Verses* that

Shōju gave his acknowledgment to the Five Ranks.

After I had entered Shōju's room and received the transmission from him, I was quite satisfied. But, though I was satisfied, I still regretted that all teachers had not yet clearly explained the meaning of " the reciprocal interpenetration of the Apparent and the Real." They seemed to have discarded the words " reciprocal interpenetration," and to pay no attention whatsoever to them. Thereupon the rhinoceros of doubt once more raised its head.

In the summer of the first year of the Kan'en era (1748-1751), in the midst of my meditation, suddenly the mystery of " the reciprocal interpenetration of the Apparent and the Real " became perfectly clear. It was just like looking at the palm of my own hand. The rhinoceros of doubt instantly fell down dead, and I could scarcely bear the joy of it. Though I wished to hand it on to others, I was ashamed to squeeze out my old woman's stinking milk and soil the monks' mouths with it.

All of you who wish to plumb this deep source must make the investigation in secret with your entire body. My own toil has extended over these thirty years. Do not take this to be an easy task! Even if you should happen to break up the family and scatter the household, do not consider this enough. You must vow to pass through seven, or eight, or even nine thickets of brambles. And, when you have passed through the thickets of brambles, still do not consider this to be enough. Vow to investigate the secret teachings of the Five Ranks to the end.

For the past eight or nine years or more, I have been trying to incite all of you who boil your daily gruel over the same fire with me to study this great matter thoroughly, but more often than not you have taken it to be the doctrine of another house, and remained indifferent to it. Only a few among you have attained understanding of it. How deeply this grieves me! Have you never heard : " The Gates of Dharma are manifold ; I vow to enter them all ?" How much the more should this be true for the main principle of Buddhism and the essential road of sanzen!

Shōju Rōjin has said: "In order to provide a means whereby students might directly experience the Four Wisdoms, the patriarchs, in their compassion and with their skill in devising expedients, first instituted the Five Ranks." What are the so-called Four Wisdoms? They are the Great Perfect Mirror Wisdom, the Universal Nature Wisdom, the Marvelous Observing Wisdom, and the Perfecting-of-Action Wisdom.

Followers of the Way, even though you may have pursued your studies in the Threefold Learning continuously through many kalpas, if you have not directly experienced the Four Wisdoms, you are not permitted to call yourselves true sons of Buddha. Followers of the Way, if your investigation has been correct and complete, at the moment you smash open the dark cave of the eighth or Ālaya consciousness, the precious light of the Great Perfect Mirror Wisdom instantly shines forth. But, strange to say, the light of the Great Perfect Mirror Wisdom is black like lacquer. This is what is called the rank of " The Apparent within the Real."

Having attained the Great Perfect Mirror Wisdom, you now enter the rank of "The Real within the Apparent." When you have accomplished your long practice of the Jeweled-mirror Samādhi, you directly realize the Universal Nature Wisdom and for the first time enter the state of the unobstructed interpenetration of Noumenon and phenomena.

But the disciple must not be satisfied here. He himself must enter into intimate acquaintance with the rank of " The Coming from within the Real." After that, by depending upon the rank of " The Arrival at Mutual Integration," he will completely prove the Marvelous Observing Wisdom and the Perfecting-of-Action Wisdom. At last he reaches the rank of " Unity Attained," and, " after all, comes back to sit among the coals and ashes."

Do you know why? Pure gold that has gone through a thousand smeltings does not become ore a second time. My only fear is that a little gain will suffice you. How priceless is the merit gained through the step-by-step practice of the Five Ranks of the Apparent and the Real! By this practice you not only attain the Four Wisdoms, but you personally prove that the Three Bodies also are wholly embraced within your own body. Have you not read in the *Daijō shōgongyō ron*: "When the eight consciousnesses are inverted, the Four Wisdoms are produced; when the Four Wisdoms are bound together, the Three Bodies are perfected?" Therefore Sōkei Daishi composed this verse:

Your own nature is provided
With the Three Bodies;
When its brightness is manifested,
The Four Wisdoms are attained.

He also said: "The pure Dharmakāya is your nature; the perfect Sambhogakāya is your wisdom; the myriad Nirmāṇakāyas are your activities."

TŌZAN RYŌKAI'S VERSES ON THE FIVE RANKS

The Apparent within the Real:
In the third watch of the night
Before the moon appears,
No wonder when we meet
There is no recognition!
Still cherished in my heart
Is the beauty of earlier days.

The rank of "The Apparent within the Real" denotes the rank of the Absolute, the rank in which one experiences the Great Death, shouts "KA!" sees Tao, and enters into the Principle. When the true practitioner, filled with power from his secret study, meritorious achievements, and hidden practices, suddenly bursts through into this rank, "the empty sky vanishes and the iron mountain crumbles." "Above, there is not a tile to cover his head; below, there is not an inch of ground for him to stand on." The delusive passions are non-existent, enlightenment is non-existent, Samsara is non-existent, Nirvana is non-existent. This is the state of total empty solidity, without sound and without odor, like a bottomless clear pool. It is as if every fleck of cloud had been wiped from the vast sky.

Too often the disciple, considering that his attainment of this rank is the end of the Great Matter and his discernment of the Buddha-way complete, clings to it to the death and will not let go of it. Such as this is called "stagnant water" Zen; such a man is called "an evil spirit who keeps watch over the corpse in the coffin." Even though he remains absorbed in this state for thirty or forty years, he will never get out of the cave of the self-complacency and inferior fruits of pratyeka-buddhahood. Therefore it is said: "He whose activity does not leave this rank sinks into the poisonous sea." He is the man whom Buddha called "the fool who gets his realization in the rank of the Real."

Therefore, though as long as he remains in this hiding place of quietude, passivity and vacantness, inside and outside are transparent and his understanding perfectly clear, the moment the bright insight [he has thus far gained through his practice] comes into contact with differentiation's defiling conditions of turmoil and confusion, agitation and vexation, love and hate, he will find himself utterly helpless before them, and all the miseries of existence will press in upon him. It was in order to save him from this serious illness that the rank of " The Real within the Apparent " was established as an expedient.

The Real within the Apparent:
A sleepy-eyed grandam
Encounters herself in an old mirror.

Clearly she sees a face,
But it doesn't resemble hers at all.
Too bad, with a muddled head,
She tries to recognize her reflection !

If the disciple had remained in the rank of "The Apparent within the Real," his judgment would always have been vacillating and his view prejudiced. Therefore, the bodhisattva of superior capacity invariably leads his daily life in the realm of the [six] dusts, the realm of all kinds of ever-changing differentiation. All the myriad phenomena before his eyes—the old and the young, the honorable and the base, halls and pavilions, verandahs and corridors, plants and trees, mountains and rivers—he regards as his own original, true, and pure aspect. It is just like looking into a bright mirror and seeing his own face in it. If he continues for a long time to observe everything everywhere with this radiant insight, all appearances of themselves become the jeweled mirror of his own house, and he becomes the jeweled mirror of their houses as well. Eihei has said: "The experiencing of the manifold dharmas through using oneself is delusion; the experiencing of oneself through the coming of the manifold dharmas is satori." This is just what I have been saying. This is the state of "mind and body discarded, discarded mind and body." It is like two mirrors mutually reflecting one another without even the shadow of an image between. Mind and the objects of mind are one and the same; things and oneself are not two. "A white horse enters the reed flowers"; "snow is piled up in a silver bowl."

This is what is known as the Jeweled-mirror Samādhi. This is what the *Nirvana Sutra* is speaking about when it says: "The Tathāgata sees the Buddha-nature with his own eyes." When you have entered this samādhi, "though you push the great white ox, he does not go away"; the Universal Nature Wisdom manifests itself before your very eyes. This is what is meant by the expressions, "There exists only one Vehicle," "the Middle Path," "the True Form," "the Supreme Truth."

But, if the student, having reached this state, were to be satisfied with it, then, as before, he would be living in the deep pit of "fixation in a lesser rank of bodhisattvahood." Why is this so? Because he is neither conversant with the deportment of the bodhisattva, nor does he understand the causal conditions for a Buddha-land. Although he has a clear understanding of the Universal and True Wisdom, he cannot cause to shine forth the Marvelous Wisdom that comprehends the unobstructed interpenetration of the manifold dharmas. The patriarchs, in order to save him from this calamity, have provided the rank of "The Coming from within the Real."

> The Coming from within the Real:
> Within nothingness there is a path
> Leading away from the dusts of the world.
> Even if you observe the taboo
> On the present emperor's name,
> You will surpass that eloquent one of yore
> Who silenced every tongue.

In this rank, the Mahayana bodhisattva does not remain in the state of attainment that he has realized, but from the midst of the sea of effortlessness he lets his great uncaused compassion shine forth. Standing upon the four pure and great Universal Vows, he lashes forward the Dharma-wheel of "seeking Bodhi above and saving sentient beings below." This is the so-called "coming-from within the going-to, the going-to within the coming-from." Moreover, he must know the moment of [the meeting of] the paired opposites, brightness and darkness. Therefore the rank of "The Arrival at Mutual Integration" has been set up.

The Arrival at Mutual Integration:
When two blades cross points,
There's no need to withdraw.
The master swordsman
Is like the lotus blooming in the fire.
Such a man has in and of himself
A heaven-soaring spirit.

In this rank, the bodhisattva of indomitable spirit turns
the Dharma-wheel of the non-duality of brightness and darkness. He stands in the midst of the filth of the world, "his
head covered with dust and his face streaked with dirt."
He moves through the confusion of sound and sensual
pleasure, buffeted this way and buffeted that. He is like
the fire-blooming lotus, that, on encountering the flames,
becomes still brighter in color and purer in fragrance.
"He enters the market place with empty hands," yet
others receive benefit from him. This is what is called
"to be on the road, yet not to have left the house; to have
left the house, yet not to be on the road." Is he an ordinary man? Is he a sage? The evil ones and the heretics
cannot discern him. Even the buddhas and the patriarchs
cannot lay their hands upon him. Were anyone to try to
indicate his mind, [it would be no more there than] the
horns of a rabbit or the hairs of a tortoise that have gone
beyond the farthest mountain.

Still, he must not consider this state to be his final
resting place. Therefore it is said, "Such a man has in
and of himself a heaven-soaring spirit." What must he
do in the end? He must know that there is one more
rank, the rank of " Unity Attained."

Unity Attained:
Who dares to equal him
Who falls into neither being nor non-being !
All men want to leave

The current of ordinary life,
But he, after all, comes back
To sit among the coals and ashes.

The Master's verse-comment says:
How many times has Tokuun, the idle old gimlet,
Not come down from the Marvelous Peak!
He hires foolish wise men to bring snow,
And he and they together fill up the well.

The student who wishes to pass through Tōzan's rank of "Unity Attained" should first study this verse.

It is of the utmost importance to study and pass through the Five Ranks, to attain penetrating insight into them, and to be totally without fixation or hesitation. But, though your own personal study of the Five Ranks comes to an end, the Buddha-way stretches endlessly and there are no tarrying places on it. The Gates of Dharma are manifold.

VIII. THE COMMANDMENTS

WITH the completion of the *goi* koans, our study of the Buddha-dharma as it has been traditionally handed down in the Zen Sect comes to an end. Only one more important question remains to be answered : How are we to conduct ourselves in our daily life so as never to violate the Buddha-dharma ? When we have fully penetrated the last of the Five Ranks we make our own the fundamental attitude of mind from which all the activities of the patriarchs have stemmed. But to live this attitude from morning to evening and from evening to morning is the ultimate aim of Zen practice. To this end we must pass through the Ten Commandments, scrutinizing them over and over, going from refinement to refinement, from minute detail to minute detail. In our daily activities, our feet walk on the real earth ; in the environment surrounding us, we meet that which it is our destiny to meet ; we are the master, we are the embodiment of the doctrine.

As for the Ten Commandments, they are the traditional

commandments handed down from the time of Shakyamuni
Buddha:

> Do not destroy life.
> Do not steal.
> Do not commit an unchaste act.
> Do not lie.
> Do not take intoxicating liquor.
> Do not report the wrong-doing of anyone
>   among the four groups.
> Do not slander another by praising yourself.
> Do not covet.
> Do not be stirred to anger.
> Do not revile the Three Treasures.

However many times we may have heard these commandments, or even recited them ourselves, it is not until we observe
them in sanzen with our fully opened Zen eye that we come
to understand their grandeur.   To live in accordance with their
words is difficult enough; to live in accordance with their deepest
meaning is an undertaking such as only our previous long practice could prepare us for.

How magnificent our religion is !   How profound the Truth
we follow !   When we obtain it, mastering it is difficult ; when
we master it, exhausting it is difficult.   When we have mastered
and exhausted it, its wondrousness is still difficult to fathom.
There is still progress to be made to reach the ultimate goal.
What is this ultimate goal ?   Daitō Kokushi devoted the twenty years he lived among the beggars under Gojō Bridge in
Kyoto to the long cultivation of his spiritual body.   Kanzan
Kokushi, founder of the Myōshin-ji, after he had gained the
essence of Daitō Kokushi's Dharma, went deep into the moun-
tainous district of Ibuka, and cultivated himself for many years.
In the daytime he worked as a hired laborer; at night he went
into his cliff dwelling and sat in quietude.   When we bring
ourselves to think about the accomplishments of the patriarchs,
and see ourselves as we are today, we cannot but feel alarmed.

In the *Hōkyō zammai* of Tōzan Ryōkai, it is said: "Hidden practice and secret activity seem stupid and foolish, but when you have succeeded to your inheritance you are called a master among masters." How many words there are that penetrate to the very marrow of our bones!

In the monasteries of the Rinzai Sect of Zen, at the beginning and middle of the summer and winter terms, and on the night before Rōhatsu Ō Sesshin, the masters read to their monks the *Kikan*, or "Admonitions," handed down through generations in each monastery. These Admonitions are important guiding principles for the monks, and words of encouragement to them in their practice. Though they are intended for monks living in a monastery, and certain of them do not apply to laymen, the underlying principles for laymen and monks are not different. The spirit in which both must undertake and carry through their practice is exactly the same; the goal toward which all are striving is the same goal. Let me select a few passages from the *Admonitions* of my monastery, Kōon-ji:

All you worthy Zen students, confronting the realm where understanding through reason does not exist, each and every one of you must summon up the koan which is his own to study, and investigate it to the limit, backward and forward. No matter what confusion and what difficulties you may encounter, you must never give up.

Do not take sanzen like a blind man. Do not haphazardly point to this and that, saying, "This is Zen," "That is satori." Explaining a thing does not hit the pivot. By real sanzen you must attain the true proof. If you do not experience satori, what are you good for?

Do not build your house upon the sand. Make your true mind the basic ground; make your resolute vows the foundation stones; make your genuine satori the measuring line; make your zazen practice the beams and the ridgepole. If you diligently and steadfastly carry on your quest with your entire being, never stopping for a moment, the day will surely come when you will attain that bright vision which is the result of your long and strenuous effort.

Be apprehensive, take heed! Exert yourselves, be on your guard!

I have spoken about the essential points in the course we students traverse in our Zen practice. Though I am sure many remain obscure and difficult for you to understand, the essence of Zen is simple. It is freedom, it is actuality, it is action, it is daily life.

For those of us who follow this religion, our journey has no end, for, though our formal practice may be completed, its final step is a rededication to the accomplishment of the Four Vows, a task continuing into eternity.

PART THREE

SELECTIONS FROM
A ZEN PHRASE ANTHOLOGY
(*ZENRIN KUSHŪ*)

A ZEN PHRASE ANTHOLOGY

ZENRIN KUSHŪ 禪林句集 A Zen Phrase Anthology, is a collection of phrases and verses well known to all students of Zen, whether they be monks or laymen.

The original of the work, entitled *Ku zōshi* 句雙紙 A Phrase Book, was compiled sometime toward the end of the 15th century by Tōyō Eichō Zenji 東陽英朝禪師 (1429–1504), a descendant in the 7th generation of Kanzan Egen, founder of the Myōshin-ji. It consisted of some 5,000 quotations taken from Buddhist sutras, the records of Chinese Zen patriarchs, Confucian texts, Taoist writings, and the works of Chinese poets. These quotations were arranged in sections according to the number of Chinese characters in each, beginning with entries of a single character, and progressing numerically through those of two, three, four characters, five characters and parallel five-character phrases, six characters and parallel six-character phrases, seven characters and parallel seven-character phrases, to those of eight characters and parallel eight-character phrases.

The collection seems to have remained in manuscript form until the latter half of the 17th century, when a person who styled himself Ijūshi 已十子, and about whom nothing is known, undertook to edit it. Ijūshi states in his postscript to the book that he was originally a Confucianist, but in middle life became a monk and carried on some Zen practice. Later, however, "due to an unfortunate circumstance," he had to return to Confucianism. Because of his desire to repay the debt of gratitude he felt toward his Zen friends, he decided to edit Eichō's work, which he believed would be useful to beginners in Zen study. To each section Ijūshi added an appendix of additional quotations, bringing the total to about 6,000 entries. Furthermore, except in the case of the few quotations whose sources he could not trace, he appended to each entry the title and section of the original work from which it had been taken. The collection was finally published in 1688 under its present title, *Zenrin kushū*.

In the two hundred and fifty odd years since the book first appeared, numerous editions have been printed, some with explanatory notes for each entry in addition to source references. A number of abbreviated versions have also been published, as well as other anthologies based upon it or resembling it and bearing similar titles. Even a kind of phrase dictionary has appeared, containing entries not included in the original work, though lacking many others. Copies of any edition of Ijūshi's text are difficult to find today, even at second hand. The most easily available of the similar works are the abridged version, *Zenrin kushū*, edited by SHIBAYAMA Zenkei, and published by Kichūdō 其中堂 in Kyoto in 1952, and the section entitled "Kushū" 句集 in *Zudokko (Zokuhen)*, pp. 173–301.

Today *Zenrin kushū*, or its equivalent, is still the constant companion of every Japanese student of sanzen, for within its thousands of phrases he must find the particular traditional *jakugo* or "capping phrase"—sometimes two or three—for the koan he is studying, and present it to his teacher as the final step in his study of the koan. Day by day and week by week, thumbing through this work, usually printed in small type on thin paper in a size convenient for the pocket or the sleeve, the student memorizes a word here and a phrase there, until his mind gradually becomes a repository for many of the famous and beautiful lines from Chinese literature.

No translation of the complete *Zenrin kushū* in any European language has as yet been published.   However, English translations of a number of the verses are to be found throughout the various English writings of D.T. SUZUKI.   *Zen in English Literature,* and *Haiku,* Vol. I, both by R. H. BLYTH, also contain English translations of some of the phrases.   Others by the Zen Master Sokei-an are scattered through *Cat's Yawn.*

The selections that follow have been chosen by Isshū Rōshi from each of the twelve sections of the anthology, and illustrate the wide variation in content and literary form to be found in it.   Sources, and, except in a few cases, explanatory notes, have been omitted.

ONE-CHARACTER PHRASES

1. 是
   Ze!
   Yes! Good! Right! Correct! All right! That's it!

2. 了
   Ryō!
   Understood! Clear! Finished! Done!

3. 點
   Ten!
   There! That's it! Just so! Check!

4. 参

San!

Reflect further! Think more deeply! Investigate more thoroughly.

Ask! Enquire!

This second usage is encountered occasionally when a master, in the course of a lecture, asks his audience to question him further.

5. 錯

Shaku!

Error! Wrong! Mistake! It doesn't hit the mark!

6. 力

Ka! or *Ga!*
Ha! Ho!

This character is found only in Zen literature, where it is most often used to indicate a spontaneous cry made at the moment of attaining satori, and thus, by inference, satori itself. It is an exclamation giving the impression of great power.

It is also a loud cry shouted rhythmically and in unison by a group of men engaged in some heavy labor, for instance, fishermen dragging their boat up onto the shore.

7. 無

Mu!
Mu!

As an exclamation, this word should not be translated. It was made famous by Jōshū Jūshin 趙州從諗 (Chao-chou Ts'ung-shên). When used as a negative it means: without, has not, ... -less; nothing, none.

8. 關

Kan!
Kan!

An untranslatable exclamation made famous by Ummon Bun'en 雲門 文偃 (Yün-mên Wên-yen), and known as one of his "One Word Barriers" (*ichijikan* 一字關 *i-tzu-kuan*). The literal meaning is: a frontier pass, a barrier which is difficult to pass through.

9. 瞎

Katsu!

Blind! Dumbell! Dunce! Ignoramus!

Used in its literal meaning, this word refers to a stupid or ignorant man. In Zen, however, it is often a complimentary term for a completely enlightened man who, to those who have no eye to see, appears to be just an everyday person with no smell of Zen about him.

10. 喝

Katsu!

Katsu!

An untranslatable exclamatory shout first given by Baso Dōitsu 馬祖 道一 (Ma-tsu Tao-i), but later made famous by Rinzai Gigen 臨濟 義玄 (Lin-chi I-hsüan) and the Rinzai School of Zen.

TWO-CHARACTER PHRASES

11. 如是

Nyoze.

Thus; like this; in this way. Just so!

12. 看看

Miyo, miyo!

Look, look! Watch out, watch out!

13. 不識

Fushiki.

[I] don't know.

14. 不會

Fue.

[I] don't understand. [I] can't understand.

15. 未在

Mizai.

Not yet.   Not at all.   Never.

16. 會也

E seri.
E su ya?

[I] understand.   [I] have understood.
Do you understand?   Have you understood?

17. 恁麼

Immo.

Thus; like this; like that; in this (or that) way.

18. 蹉過

Saka or *shaka.*

To pass by without recognition.   To miss a person, or a chance.   To slip from the right way.

19. 珍重

Chinchō!

Farewell!   Good-bye!   Take care of yourself!

A phrase used at parting.

20. 休去

Kyū shisaru.

To have been silenced; to have been caused to cease (speaking).   Not to continue further.

The implication always inherent in this phrase is that the person who ceases speaking agrees with, or is forced to accept, what has just been said by the other.

THREE-CHARACTER PHRASES

21. 鐵酸餡

    Tessan'an.

    Iron sour-stuffing.

    > Something you can't get your teeth into. Also a term of abuse.

22. 看脚下

    Kyakka o miyo!

    Look where you're going! Watch where you step!

23. 野狐精

    Yakozei.

    A wild fox spirit.

    > Used as a term of abuse.

24. 露堂堂

    Rodōdō.

    Apparent; perfectly clear. Revealed!

25. 惺惺著

    Seiseijaku!

    Be clever! Be astute! Be alert!

26. 是什麼

    Kore nanzo?

    What's this?

    > An expression usually employed when referring to a thing. When used for a person it is a term of abuse.

85

27. 信不及

Shinfugyū.

To lack self-reliance; to lack faith in oneself. To be unable to believe.

28. 可惜許

Kashakko!

Too bad! What a pity! What a shame! Regrettable!

29. 喫茶去

Kissako!

Go drink your tea!

30. 莫妄想

Maku mōzō!

Don't be deluded!

FOUR-CHARACTER PHRASES

31. 柳綠花紅

Yanagi wa midori, hana wa kurenai.

The willows are green, the flowers are red.

32. 獨步丹霄

Tanshō ni doppo su.

I alone walk in the red heavens.

33. 失錢遭罪

Shissen sōzai.

To lose one's money and incur punishment as well.

34. 再犯不容

Saibon yurusazu.

A second offense is not permitted.

35. 識法者懼

Hō o shiru mono wa osoru.

He who knows the law fears it.

36. 自領出去

Zuryō shukko.

To take what's coming to you and get out.

37. 知而故犯

Shitte kotosara ni okasu.

To know, yet deliberately to transgress.

38. 活潑潑地

Kappatsupatsuji or *kappappatchi.*

Briskly and spiritedly.

39. 認賊爲子

Zoku o mitomete ko to nasu.

To acknowledge a thief as one's child.

40. 掩耳偷鈴

Mimi o ōte suzu o nusumu.

To cover one's ears and steal the bell.

41. 言語道斷

Gongo dōdan.

Words fail.

42. 笑裏藏鋒
    Shōri ni hokosaki o zō su.
    To hide a spear within a smile.

43. 呑吐不下
    Dondo fuge.
    It can't be swallowed, it can't be spit out.

44. 龍頭蛇尾
    Ryūtō dabi.
    A dragon's head and a snake's tail.
    > That is, a good beginning and a poor ending.

45. 靈龜曳尾
    Reiki o o hiku.
    The sacred tortoise drags its tail.

46. 破家散宅
    Hake santaku.
    The family is broken up, the house destroyed.

47. 癩兒牽伴
    Raiji han o hiku.
    The leper drags his friends along with him.

48. 勞而無功
    Rō shite kō nashi.
    To work hard and accomplish nothing.

49. 落草不少
    Rakusō sukunakarazu.
    He's fallen deep in the weeds.

50. 賓主歷然
Hinju rekinen.
Guest and host are clearly distinguishable.

FIVE-CHARACTER PHRASES

51. 溪梅一朶香
Keibai ichida kambashi.
Fragrant, the valley's single plum flower.

52. 步步清風起
Hoho seifū okoru.
At every step the pure wind rises.

53. 好事不如無
Kōzu mo naki ni wa shikazu.
Even a good thing isn't so good as nothing.

54. 自屎不覺臭
Jishi kusaki o oboezu.
He doesn't recognize the smell of his own dung.

55. 憐兒不覺醜
Ji o awarende minikuki o oboezu.
A beloved son is not ugly.

56. 剜好肉作瘡
Kōniku o egutte kizu to nasu.
To gouge out healthy flesh and make a wound.

57. 能使得爺錢

Yoku yasen o tsukai etari.

He made good use of his father's money.

58. 壺中日月長

Kochū jitsugetsu nagashi.

In the pot sun and moon shine eternally.

> Once upon a time there was a hermit who always carried about
> with him a pot that could hold a peck of rice. At night he slept
> in the pot. Sometimes the pot changed into the universe with
> the sun and moon in it. He named the pot " Pot Heaven," and
> he himself was known as Mr. Pot.

59. 鑊湯無冷處

Kakutō ni reisho nashi.

There's no cool spot in a cauldron of boiling water.

60. 蝦跳不出斗

Ka odoredomo, tō o idezu.

Though the frog leaps, it can't get out of the bushel.

61. 貧兒思舊債

Hinji kyūsai o omou.

The poor man thinks about his unpaid debts.

62. 泥裏洗土塊

Deiri ni dokai o arau.

To wash a clod of earth in the mud.

63. 室內一盞燈

Shitsunai issan no tō.

The single-saucer lamp within the room.

64. 好語不說盡

Kōgo tokitsukusazare.

In a good talk, don't explain everything.

65. 按牛頭喫草

Gozu o anjite kusa o kisseshimu.

Pushing down the ox's head, he makes it eat grass.

66. 巧匠不留跡

Kōshō ato o todomezu.

A skillful craftsman leaves no traces.

67. 地肥茄子大

Chi koete nasubi dai nari.

When the earth is fertile, the eggplants are large.

68. 特地一場愁

Tokuji ichijō no urei.

The extremity of grief.

69. 聖朝無棄物

Seichō ni kibutsu nashi.

There is no waste in the Imperial Court.

70. 白雲抱幽石

Hakuun yūseki o idaku.

White clouds hold lonely rocks in their embrace.

PARALLEL FIVE-CHARACTER PHRASES

71. 掬水月在手
弄花香滿衣

Mizu o kiku sureba, tsuki te ni ari;
Hana o rō sureba, ka e ni mitsu.

Scoop up water, and the moon is in your hands;
Toy with flowers, and their fragrance scents your garments.

72. 泣露千般草
吟風一樣松

Tsuyu ni naku sempan no kusa,
Kaze ni ginzu ichiyō no matsu.

A thousand grasses weep tears of dew,
A single pine tree murmurs in the breeze.

73. 覓火和烟得
擔泉帶月歸

Hi o motomete wa kemuri ni washite e;
Izumi o ninatte wa tsuki o obite kaeru.

Seeking fire, you find it with smoke;
Carrying spring-water, you bring it back with the moon.

74. 林下十年夢
湖邊一笑新

Rinka jūnen no yume!
Kohen isshō arata nari.

Ten years of dreams in the forest!
Now on the lake's edge laughing,
Laughing a new laugh.

75. 十方無壁落
    四面又無門

Jippō hekiraku naku,
Shimen mata mon nashi.

The ten directions are without walls,
The four quarters are without gates.

76. 誰知遠烟浪
    別有好思量

Tare ka shiru tōki enrō ni
Betsu ni kōshiryō aru koto o?

Who can know that far off in the misty waves
Another yet more excellent realm of thought exists?

77. 十年歸不得
    忘却來時道

Jūnen kaeru koto o ezu,
Raiji no michi o bōkyaku su.

For ten years I couldn't return;
Now I've forgotten the road by which I came.

78. 只可自怡悅
    不堪持贈君

Tada mizukara ietsu subeshi,
Ji shite kimi ni okuru ni taezu.

Only I myself can enjoy it;
It is not suitable to present to you.

79. 泉聲中夜後
    山色夕陽時

Sensei chūya no nochi,
Sanshoku sekiyō no toki.

The murmuring of the spring as the night deepens,
The coloring of the hills as the sun goes down.

80. 陰陽不到處
    一片好風光

In'yō futō no tokoro
Ippen no kōfūkō.

Where the sun and moon do not reach,
There is marvelous scenery indeed!

81. 高捲吟中箔
    濃煎睡後茶

Takaku ginchū no sudare o maite;
Komayaka ni suigo no cha o senzu.

Singing his poem, he rolls the bamboo blind high;
Having finished his nap, he parches the tea leaves dark.

82. 枯木裏龍吟
    髑髏裏眼睛

Kobokuri no ryūgin,
Dokurori no gansei.

The dragon-hum in the dead tree,
The eyeball in the dry skull.

83. 幽鳥語喃喃
    辭雲入亂峯

Yūchō go nannan,
Kumo o ji shite rampō ni iru.

A hidden bird twitters " Nam, nam."
Taking leave of the clouds, I enter the scattered peaks.

84. 秋風吹渭水
    落葉滿長安

Shūfū Isui o fukeba,
Rakuyō Chōan ni mitsu.

94

Autumn wind, blowing over the waters of the Wei,
Covers all Ch'ang-an with falling leaves.

85. 微風吹幽松
    近聽聲愈好

Bifū yūshō o fuki,
Chikaku kikeba, koe iyo-iyo yoshi.

A light breeze stirs the lonely pine,
The sound is more pleasant heard from close by.

86. 皮膚脫落盡
    唯有一眞實

Hifu datsuraku shitsukushite
Tada ichi shinjitsu nomi ari.

Now that I've shed my skin completely,
One true reality alone exists.

87. 能爲萬象主
    不逐四時凋

Yoku banzō no shu to natte,
Shiji o otte shibomazu.

When you're really master of the myriad forms,
Throughout the four seasons there's no withering, no decay.

88. 相逢相不識
    共語不知名

Aiōte aishirazu,
Tomo ni katatte na o shirazu.

I meet him, but know not who he is;
I converse with him, but do not know his name.

89. 隨流認得性
　　無喜亦無憂

Nagare ni shitagatte shō o nintoku sureba,
Ki mo naku mata yū mo nashi.

When you recognize [Mind's] nature while according with
　its flow,
There's no more joy, nor is there any sorrow.

90. 一華開五葉
　　結果自然成

Ikka goyō hiraite
Kekka ji'nen ni naru.

The five petals of the one flower open,
And the fruit of itself is ripe.

SIX-CHARACTER PHRASES

91. 前三三後三三

Zen sansan, go sansan.

Before, three times three,
Behind, three times three.

92. 痴兀兀兀兀痴

Chi gotsugotsu, gotsugotsu chi.

Stupidly steadfast, steadfastly stupid.

93. 懸羊頭賣狗肉

Yōtō o kakete kuniku o uru.

He displays a sheep's head but sells dog flesh.

96

94. 井覷驢驢覷井

Sei ro o mi, ro sei o miru.

The well looks at the ass,
The ass looks at the well.

95. 倒騎牛入佛殿

Sakashima ni ushi ni notte butsuden ni iru.

Riding backwards on an ox,
I enter the Buddha-hall.

96. 好兒不使爺錢

Kōji yasen o tsukawazu.

A good son doesn't use his father's money.

97. 面赤不如語直

Men no akakaran yori wa, go no naokaran ni wa shikazu.

Honest speech is better than a red face.

98. 嗔拳不打笑面

Shinken shōmen o da sezu.

An angry fist does not strike a smiling face.

99. 鉢裏飯桶裏水

Hatsurihan, tsūrisui.

Rice in the bowl, water in the bucket.

100. 無孔笛最難吹

Mukuteki mottomo fukigatashi.

The flute without holes is the most difficult to blow.

101. 三人證龜作鼈

Sannin kame o shō shite betsu to nasu.

Three men testified about the tortoise, so that makes it a turtle.

> A wise man once said: "If a man told you he had seen a tiger in the street, you wouldn't believe him. If a second man said the same thing, you wouldn't believe him either. But if a third man said he also had seen one, you'd believe that there had been a tiger in the street."

102. 臂膊不向外曲

Hihaku soto ni mukatte magarazu.

The arm doesn't bend outward.

103. 入地獄如箭射

Jigoku ni iru koto ya no iru ga gotoshi.

Going to hell with the speed of an arrow.

104. 聞名不如見面

Na o kikan yori wa omote o min ni wa shikazu.

Better to see the face than to hear the name.

105. 烟霞不遮梅香

Enka baikō o saegirazu.

The hazy mist does not stay
The plum flower's fragrance.

106. 家醜莫向外揚

Kashū soto ni mukatte aguru koto nakare.

Don't display the family skeletons in public.

107. 跨瞎驢追猛虎

Katsuro ni notte mōko o ou.

Astride a blind ass he pursues a fierce tiger.

108. 急水上打毬子

Kyūsuijō ni kyūsu o da su.

He's hitting at a ball on swift-flowing water.

109. 良賈深藏如虛

Ryōko wa fukaku zō shite munashiki ga gotoshi.

The good merchant hides his possessions well and appears
  to have nothing.

110. 藏頭白海頭黑

Zōzu haku, Kaizu koku.

Mr. Tsang's head is white, Mr. Hai's head is black.

PARALLEL SIX-CHARACTER PHRASES

111. 認箇照照靈靈
  落在驢前馬後

Kono shōshō reirei o mitomete,
Rozen bago ni rakuzai su.

Believing this to be radiance and spirituality, he is content
  to run in front of asses and follow after horses.

112. 寒時寒殺闍梨
  熱時熱殺闍梨

Kanji wa jari o kansatsu shi,
Netsuji wa jari o nessatsu su.

The cold kills you with cold, the heat kills you with heat.

113. 上無片瓦蓋頭
  下無寸土立足

Kami henga no kōbe o ōu naku,
Shimo sundo no ashi o rissuru nashi.

Above, there isn't a piece of tile to cover his head; below
there isn't an inch of earth for him to stand on.

114. 口 欲 談 而 辭 喪
心 欲 緣 而 慮 忘

Kuchi danzen to hosshite ji sō shi;
Kokoro enzen to hosshite ryo bōzu.

When the mouth wants to speak about it, words fail;
when the mind seeks affinity with it, thought vanishes.

115. 日 月 照 臨 不 到
天 地 蓋 覆 不 盡

Jitsugetsu mo shōrin shi itarazu;
Tenchi mo gaifuku shitsukusazu.

Sun and moon cannot illumine it completely; heaven and
earth cannot cover it entirely.

116. 雖 與 我 同 條 生
不 與 我 同 條 死

Ware to dōjō ni shōzu to iedomo,
Ware to dōjō ni shi sezu.

Though we're born of the same lineage, we don't die of
the same lineage.

117. 相 罵 饒 你 接 觜
相 唾 饒 你 潑 水

Ainonoshiru koto wa nanji ni yurusu kuchibashi o tsuge;
Aida suru koto wa nanji ni yurusu mizu o sosoge.

When we're reviling one another, you may give me tit for
tat; when we're spitting at one another, you may spew
me with slobber.

118. 逐鹿者不見山
　　　攫金者不見人

Shika o ou mono wa yama o mizu,
Kin o tsukamu mono wa hito o mizu.

The deer-hunter doesn't see the mountains, the miser doesn't see men.

119. 達磨不來東土
　　　二祖不往西天

Daruma Tōdo ni kitarazu,
Niso Seiten ni yukazu.

Bodhidharma didn't come to China, the Second Patriarch didn't go to India.

120. 入息不居陰界
　　　出息不涉萬緣

Nissoku onkai ni kyo sezu,
Shussoku ban'en ni watarazu.

Breathing in, he does not stay in the realm of the skandhas; breathing out, he is not concerned with the myriad things.

121. 去年貧未是貧
　　　今年貧始是貧

Kyonen no hin wa imada kore hin narazu,
Konnen no hin wa hajimete kore hin.

Last year's poverty was not real poverty,
But this year's poverty is poverty indeed.

122. 諸天捧花無路
　　　外道潛覬不見

Shoten hana o sasaguru ni michi naku,
Gedō hisoka ni miru ni miezu.

101

The devas find no path on which to strew flowers; the heretics secretly spying find nothing to see.

123. 離婁不辨正色
　　 師曠豈識玄絲

Ri Rō shōshiki o benzezu;
Shi Kō ani genshi o shiran ya?

Even Li Lou cannot discern the true form;
How, then, can Shih K'uang distinguish the subtle tune?

> Li Lou (Ri Rō) and Shih K'uang (Shi Kō) were both men of ancient times. The former was famous for his sharp eyesight, the latter for his sharp hearing.

124. 去年梅今歳柳
　　 顔色馨香依舊

Kyonen no ume konsai no yanagi—
Ganshoku keikō kyū ni yoru.

Last year's plum and this year's willow—
Their color and fragrance are as of old.

125. 坐斷毘盧頂顇
　　 曾不見有佛祖

Biru chōnei o zadan shite
Katsute busso aru koto o mizu.

Having cut off the top of Vairocana's head, I don't know that any buddha or patriarch ever existed.

126. 天際日上月下
　　 檻前山深水寒

Tensai hi nobori tsuki kudaru,
Kanzen yama fukaku mizu samushi.

At the limits of heaven the sun rises and the moon sets,
Beyond the balustrade the mountains deepen and the waters

become chill.

127. 只見溪回路轉
不知身在桃源

Tada kei meguri michi tenzuru o mite,
Shirazu mi no tōgen ni aru koto o.

He sees only the winding of the stream and the twisting
of the path,
He does not know that already he is in the land of the
immortals.

128. 欲識佛性義理
當觀時節因緣

Busshō no giri o shiran to hosseba
Masa ni jisetsu innen o kanzu beshi.

He who would understand the meaning of Buddha-nature
Must watch for the season and the causal relations.

129. 一切聲是佛聲
一切色是佛色

Issai no koe wa kore busshō,
Issai no iro wa kore busshiki.

Every voice is the voice of Buddha, every form is the
Buddha-form.

130. 雁無遺蹤之意
水無沈影之心

Kari ni ishō no i naku,
Mizu ni chin'ei no kokoro nashi.

The wild goose has no intention of leaving traces, the water
has no thought of engulfing reflections.

SEVEN-CHARACTER PHRASES

131. 說似一物即不中

Setsuji ichimotsu soku fuchū.

The instant you speak about a thing you miss the mark.

132. 燕雀何知鴻鵠志

Enjaku nanzo kōkō no kokorozashi o shiran ya?

How can the mountain-finch know the wild swan's aspiring?

133. 八角磨盤空裏走

Hakkaku no maban kūri ni washiru.

The eight-cornered mortar rushes across the sky.

134. 狸奴白牯放毫光

Ri'nu byakko gōkō o hanatsu.

The badger and the white bull emit a glorious radiance.

135. 一鳥不鳴山更幽

Itchō nakazu yama sara ni yū nari.

With no bird singing
The mountain is yet more still.

136. 枯木花開劫外春

Koboku hana hiraku gōgai no haru.

In the spring beyond time
The withered tree flowers.

137. 鷺鷥立雪非同色

Roji yuki ni tatsu, dōshoku ni arazu.

When the snowy heron stands in the snow, the colors are
   not the same.

138. 再來不直半文錢

Sairai hammonsen ni atarazu.

A second try is not worth half a cash.

139. 兩箇猢猻探水月

Ryōko no koson suigetsu o saguru.

A pair of monkeys are reaching
For the moon in the water.

140. 爲君幾下蒼龍窟

Kimi ga tame ni ikutabi ka sōryōkutsu ni kudaru.

How many times for your sake
Have I not gone down into the blue dragon's cave!

141. 入火眞金色轉鮮

Hi ni itte shinkin iro utata azayaka nari.

When pure gold enters the fire,
Its color becomes still brighter.

142. 遠山無限碧層層

Enzan kagiri naku hekisōsō.

Endlessly rise the distant mountains,
Blue heaped upon blue.

143. 明月蘆花君自看

Meigetsu roka kimi mizukara miyo.

You must see for yourself
The reed-flowers drenched in moonlight.

144. 星在秤兮不在盤

Hoshi wa shō ni atte ban ni arazu.

The marks are on the balance-arm,
Not on the scale-pan.

145. 自笑一聲天地驚

Jishō isshō tenchi odoroku.

My single peal of laughter
Startles heaven and earth.

146. 針鋒頭上翻筋斗

Shimpō tōjō ni kinto o hirugaesu.

To turn a somersault on a needle's point.

147. 多口阿師難下觜

Taku no ashi kuchibashi o kudashi gatashi.

The garrulous reverend can't open his trap.

148. 一回舉著一回新

Ikkai kojaku sureba, ikkai arata nari.

Each time you bring it up,
Each time it is new.

149. 鼠入錢筒伎已窮

Nezumi sentō ni itte gi sude ni kiwamaru.

The rat that entered the money box is at its wit's end.

In old China, a bamboo tube, open only at one end and its diameter that of the coins to be stored in it, was used for a money box.

150. 千古萬古與人看

Senko banko hito no tame ni misu.

Eternally and everlastingly
It is revealing itself to men.

PARALLEL SEVEN-CHARACTER PHRASES

151. 泉州白家酒三盞
喫了猶言未沾脣

Senshū Hakke no sake sansan,
Kisshi owatte nao iu, imada kuchibiru o uruosazu to.

You've drunk three cups of wine
At the house of Pai in Ch'üan-chou,
And yet you still declare,
" My lips aren't even moistened."

152. 水自竹邊流出冷
風從花裏過來香

Mizu wa chikuhen yori ryūshutsu shite hiyayaka ni,
Kaze wa kari yori sugikitatte kambashi.

Water from the edge of the bamboos
Flows out refreshing,
Breeze from the heart of the flowers
Passes by fragrant.

153. 湘潭雲盡暮山出
巴蜀雪消春水來

Shōtan kumo tsukite bozan ide,
Hashoku yuki kiete shunsui kitaru.

107

When Hsiang-t'an's clouds disperse,
The evening mountains appear;
When Pa-shu's snows vanish,
The spring waters flow.

154. 鴛鴦繡出從君看
　　 莫把金針度與人

En'ō o nuiidashite kimi ga miru ni makasu,
Kinshin o totte hito ni doyo suru koto nakare.

The mandarin ducks I've embroidered
I give you leave to look at,
But the golden needle that made them
Do not pass on to men.

155. 三級浪高魚化龍
　　 痴人猶戽夜塘水

Sankyū nami takō shite uo ryū ni ke su,
Chijin nao kumu yatō no mizu.

Waves at the Yü Gate have risen
And the fish become dragons,
Yet fools still scoop out
The embankment's dank water.

> In ancient times King Yü 禹 of the Hsia 夏 dynasty cut a three-
> tiered sluice through the Lung-mên 龍門 mountains on the border
> between Shensi and Shansi provinces to open up a passage for
> the Yellow River. This was known as the Gate of Yü or the
> Dragon Gate. There is an old legend that, on the third day of
> the third month, when the peach trees are in flower, vigorous carp
> that could scale this three-tiered waterfall would become dragons.

156. 江上晚來堪畫處
　　 漁人披得一蓑歸

Kōjō banrai egaku ni taetaru tokoro;
Gyojin issa o hi shiete kaeru.

Evening near the riverside—
A scene for a painter.
Throwing on his straw raincoat,
The fisherman returns home.

157. 尋常一樣窓前月
纔有梅花便不同

Yonotsune ichiyō sōzen no tsuki,
Wazuka ni baika areba, sunawachi onajikarazu.

The moon outside my window
Is usually the same moon,
But as soon as there are plum flowers
It becomes a different moon.

158. 安禪不必須山水
滅却心頭火自涼

Anzen wa kanarazu shimo sansui o mochiizu;
Shintō mekkyaku sureba, hi mo onozukara suzushi.

No need at all of hills and streams
For quiet meditation;
When the mind has been extinguished,
Even fire is refreshing.

159. 猿抱子歸青嶂後
鳥啣花落碧岩前

Saru ko o idaite seishō no ushiro ni kaeri;
Tori hana o fukunde hekigan no mae ni otsu.

The monkeys, clasping their young to their breasts,
Return behind the blue peaks;
A bird, holding a flower in its beak,
Alights before the green grotto.

160. 榔標橫擔不顧人
直入千峯萬峯去

Sokuritsu ō ni ninatte hito o kaerimizu,
Jiki ni sempō bampō ni irisaru.

With his staff across his back,
He pays no heed to men;
Quickly entering the myriad peaks,
He goes upon his way.

161. 只見落紅風拂盡
豈知庭樹綠陰多

Tada rakkō kaze no haraitsukusu o miru;
Ani teiju ryokuin no ōki koto o shiran ya?

I saw merely fallen petals
Blown away by the wind;
How could I know that the garden trees'
Green shadows are many?

162. 凜凜孤風不自誇
端居寰海定龍蛇

Rinrin taru kofū mizukara hokorazu;
Kankai ni tango shite ryōda o sadamu.

Fearsome and solitary in mien,
He does not boast of himself;
But, dwelling gravely in his domain,
Decides who is snake, who is dragon.

163. 江國春風吹不起
鷓鴣啼在深花裏

Kōkoku no shumpū fukitatazu,
Shako naite shinka no uchi ni ari.

Over the river country
Spring winds are not stirring,
From within the deep flowers
The partridges cry.

164. 有意氣時添意氣
不風流處也風流

Iki aru toki iki o soe;
Fūryū narazaru tokoro mata fūryū.

When your spirit is high,
Augment your spirit.
Where there is no style,
There is also some style.

165. 白鷺下田千點雪
黃鶯上樹一枝花

Hakuro ta ni kudaru senten no yuki;
Kōō ki ni noboru isshi no hana.

Snowy herons alighting in a field—
Thousands of snowflakes!
Yellow nightingales perching in a tree—
A flower-decked bough.

166. 約臂黃金寬一寸
逢人猶道不相思

Hiji ni yaku suru ōgon yuruki koto issun,
Hito ni ōte wa nao iu aiomowazu to.

The golden bracelet on her arm
Is too loose by an inch,
Yet on meeting one she merely says:
" No, I'm not in love."

167. 荷葉團團團似鏡

菱角尖尖尖似錐

Kayō dandan to shite kagami yori mo madoka ni,
Ryōkaku sensen to shite kiri yori mo surudoshi.

Lotus leaves are round,
Rounder even than a mirror;
Water-chestnut horns are sharp,
Sharper even than a gimlet.

168. 沒底藍兒盛白月

無心椀子貯清風

Mottei ranji ni byakugetsu o mori,
Mushin wansu ni seifū o takuwau.

In the bottomless bamboo basket
I put the white moon;
In the bowl of mindlessness
I store the pure breeze.

169. 自携瓶去沽村酒

却著衫來作主人

Mizukara hei o tazusaesatte sonshu o kai;
Kaette san o tsukekitatte shujin to naru.

He himself took the jar
And bought the village wine;
Now he dons a robe
And makes himself the host.

170. 竹影掃堦塵不動

月穿潭底水無痕

Chikuei kai o haratte chiri ugokazu,
Tsuki tantei o ugatte mizu ni ato nashi.

Bamboo shadows sweep the stairs,
Yet not a mote of dust is stirred;
Moonbeams pierce to the bottom of the pool,
Yet in the water not a trace remains.

EIGHT-CHARACTER PHRASES

171. 金屑雖貴落眼成翳

Kinsetsu tattoshi to iedomo, manako ni ochite ei to naru.

Though gold-dust is precious, in the eyes it obscures the vision.

172. 朝打三千暮打八百

Chōda sanzen, boda happyaku.

Three thousand blows in the morning, eight hundred blows in the evening.

173. 好雪片片不落別處

Kōsetsu hempen, bessho ni ochizu.

Lovely snowflakes, they fall nowhere else!

174. 龜上覓毛兎邊求角

Kijō ni ke o motome, tohen ni tsuno o motomu.

To look for hair on the back of a tortoise or seek for horns on the head of a rabbit.

175. 石人點頭露柱拍手

Sekijin tentō sureba, rochū te o haku su.

When the stone man nods his head, the wooden pillar claps its hands.

176. 針頭削鐵鷺股割肉

Shintō ni tetsu o kezuri, roko ni niku o saku.

To shave iron from a needle-point; to hack flesh from a heron's leg.

177. 垂絲千尺意在深潭

Suishi senjaku, i shintan ni ari.

When I drop the line down a thousand feet, my objective lies in the depths of the pool.

178. 鷄寒上樹鴨寒下水

Niwatori samū shite ki ni nobori, kamo samū shite mizu ni kudaru.

When chickens are cold they roost in a tree; when ducks are cold they dive into the water.

179. 眞不掩僞曲不藏直

Shin gi o ōwazu, kyoku choku o kakusazu.

The true does not conceal the false, the bent does not hide the straight.

180. 快人一言快馬一鞭

Kaijin ichigen, kaiba ichiben.

To the intelligent man, one word; to the fleet horse, one flick of the whip.

181. 弄泥團漢有什麼限

Deidan o rō suru no kan, nan no kagiri ka aran?

When will the fellow who plays with dirt ever have done!

182. 凡聖同居龍蛇混雜

Bonshō dōgo, ryōda konzatsu.

Laymen and holy men dwell together, dragons and snakes intermingle.

183. 官不容針私通車馬

Kan ni wa hari mo irezu, watakushi ni wa shaba o tsūzu.

Officially, a needle is not permitted to pass; unofficially, carriages can get through.

184. 蚌含明月兎子懷胎

Bō meigetsu o fukumi, toshi kaitai su.

The oyster holds a moonbeam in its mouth, the rabbit cherishes a child in its womb.

> In ancient China it was believed that pearls are created by the entrance of a moonbeam into the aperture in an oyster's shell, and that a rabbit becomes pregnant when it looks at the full moon.

185. 入火不燒入水不溺

Hi ni itte mo yakezu, mizu ni itte mo oborezu.

Entering fire he is not burned, entering water he is not drowned.

186. 朝到西天暮歸東土

Ashita ni wa Seiten ni itari, kure ni wa Tōdo ni kaeru.

In the morning he reaches India,
In the evening he returns to China.

187. 吞舟魚不遊數仞谷

Donshū no uo wa sūjin no tani ni asobazu.

A fish that can swallow a boat doesn't swim around in a valley stream.

188. 巢父飲牛許由洗耳

Sōfu ushi ni mizukai, Kyo Yū mimi o arau.

Ch'ao-fu waters his ox, Hsü Yu washes his ears.

> Ch'ao-fu (Sōfu) and Hsü Yu (Kyo Yū) were two men of ancient China, famous for their spotless integrity. When the Emperor Yao 堯 (*trad.* B.C. 2357) offered his throne to Hsü Yu, the latter is said to have hurried off to wash his ears in the stream in order to cleanse them of defilement. Ch'ao-fu, hearing of this, led his ox upstream to drink so that it would not be contaminated by the water in which Hsü Yu had washed his ears.

189. 不慕諸聖不重己靈

Shoshō o shitawazu, korei o omonzezu.

I do not emulate the sages; I do not esteem my own spirit.

190. 天上天下唯我獨尊

Tenjō tenge yuiga dokuson.

In heaven and on earth, I alone am to be revered.

PARALLEL EIGHT-CHARACTER PHRASES

191. 劍輪飛處日月沈輝
     寶杖敵時乾坤失色

Kenrin tobu tokoro, jitsugetsu hikari o shizume;
Hōjō teki suru toki, kenkon iro o shissu.

When the sword-disc flies,
Sun and moon darken;
When the jewel-staff strikes,
Heaven and earth pale.

192. 爐鞴之所鈍鐵猶多
     良醫之門病者愈甚

Rohai no tokoro dontetsu nao ōku,
Ryōi no mon byōsha iyo-iyo hanahadashi.

In the blacksmith's shop there are still piles of blunt iron;
at the good physician's gate more and more sick men
wait.

193 · 孤峰頂上目視雲霄
古渡頭邊和泥合水

Kohō chōjō manako ni unshō o mi,
Koto tōhen wadei gassui.

From the top of the solitary peak,
I gaze at the clouds;
Close by the old ferry landing,
I am splashed with mire.

194. 冬至月頭賣被買牛
冬至月尾賣牛買被

Tōji gettō ni aru toki, hi o utte ushi o kai;
Tōji getsubi ni aru toki, ushi o utte hi o kau.

On the first day of winter
I sell my quilt and buy an ox;
On the last day of winter
I sell my ox and buy a quilt.

195. 追大鵬於藕絲竅中
納須彌於蟭螟眼裏

Taihō o gūshi kyōchū ni oi;
Shumi o shōmei ganri ni iru.

To pursue the Great Roc into the tube of a lotus stem; to
put Mount Sumeru into the eye of a midge.

117

196. 姑蘇臺畔不語春秋
　　 衲僧面前豈論玄妙

Koso daihan shunjū o katarazu;
Nōsō menzen ani gemmyō o ronzen ya?

On the Ku-su Terrace
We do not speak of *The Spring and Autumn.*
In front of my face
How can you discuss the profoundly mysterious!

> The terrace was a pleasure pavilion built by King Fu-ch'a of Wu
> 吳夫差 for his beautiful concubine Hsi-shih 西施. Its ruins were
> used in Chinese poetry as a metaphor for the inevitable fall of
> pomp and power. *The Spring and Autumn* is an historical
> work traditionally said to have been edited by Confucius in such
> a way as to pass moral judgment on the men and events recorded
> in it.

197. 欲能其詩先能其心
　　 欲能其畫先能其容

*Sono shi o yoku sen to hosseba, mazu sono kokoro o yoku
shi;*
Sono ga o yoku sen to hosseba, mazu sono yō o yoku seyo.

If you want to write such a poem, you must first be capable
of such a mind; if you want to paint such a picture, you
must first be capable of grasping such a form.

198. 漁歌烟浦咸稱富貴
　　 樵唱雲樹共樂昇平

Gyo wa empo ni utatte, mina fūki to shō shi,
Shō wa unju ni tonaete, tomo ni shōhei o tanoshimu.

The fishermen singing on the misty shore
All extol good fortune and honor;
The woodcutters chanting among the lofty trees
Together rejoice in the era of peace.

199. 若也會得入鄉隨俗
若也不會餓死首陽

Moshi mata etoku seba, kyō ni itte zoku ni shitagau;
Moshi mata e sezumba, Shuyō ni gashi sen.

If you can understand, you will return to your village and
become a rustic; if you cannot understand, you will
starve on Shou-yang.

When King Wu of Chou 周武王 overthrew the Yin 殷 dynasty,
the two brothers Po I 伯夷 and Shu Ch'i 叔齊, heirs to a feudal
kingdom under the Yin, condemned him as a rebel and, refusing
to "eat the grain of Chou," withdrew to a mountain called Shou-
yang (Shuyō), where, with only ferns for food, they eventually
starved to death.

200. 孤峯頂上嘯月眠雲
大洋海中翻波走浪

Kohō chōjō tsuki ni usobuki kumo ni nemuru;
Taiyō kaichū nami o hirugaeshi nami o hashirasu.

On the top of the solitary peak,
He whistles at the moon and sleeps in the clouds;
Within the vast ocean,
He overturns the waves and rouses the breakers.

201. 天與不取反受其咎
時至不行反受其殃

Ten no atauru o torazareba, kaette sono toga o uku;
Toki itatte okonawazareba, kaette sono wazawai o uku.

Not to take what Heaven gives is to incur Heaven's
calamity; not to act when the moment comes is to incur
Heaven's misfortune.

202. 白雲堆裏不見白雲
流水聲裏不聞流水

Hakuun tairi hakuun o mizu;
Ryūsui seiri ryūsui o kikazu.

119

Enwrapped in billows of white clouds, I do not see the
white clouds; absorbed in the sound of flowing water,
I do not hear the flowing water.

203. 堯風蕩蕩野老謳歌
舜日熙熙漁人鼓棹

Gyōfū tōtō to shite yarō ōka shi;
Shunjitsu kiki to shite gyojin sao o ko su.

When Yao's influence spread throughout the land,
The peasants sang their songs;
When Shun's radiance shone o'er his vast domain,
The fishermen drummed with their oars.

> Yao (Gyō) and Shun were Sage Emperors in the golden age of
> China.

204. 以盲爲明以聾爲聰
以危爲安以吉爲凶

Mō o motte myō to nashi, rō o motte sō to nashi;
Ki o motte an to nashi, kitsu o motte kyō to nasu.

I take blindness as vision, deafness as hearing;
I take danger as safety and prosperity as misfortune.

205. 隔山見煙便知是火
隔墻見角便知是牛

Yama o hedatete kemuri o mireba, sunawachi kore hi
naru koto o shiri;
Kaki o hedatete tsuno o mireba, sunawachi kore ushi
naru koto o shiru.

When I see smoke beyond the mountain I know there's a
fire; when I see horns beyond the fence I know there's
an ox.

206. 欲透塵勞須知要徑
將施妙藥先候病原

Jinrō o tōran to hosseba, subekaraku yōkei o shiru beshi;
Masa ni myōyaku o hodokosan to seba, mazu byōgen o
ukagau.

To pass through the dusty turmoil of the world you must
know the main road; to dispense healing medicine you
must first enquire into the source of the illness.

207. 凡夫若知即是聖人
聖人若會即是凡夫

Bompu moshi shiraba, sunawachi kore seijin;
Seijin moshi e seba, sunawachi kore bompu.

When an ordinary man attains knowledge he is a sage;
when a sage attains understanding he is an ordinary man.

208. 鸚鵡能言不離飛鳥
猩猩能言不離禽獸

Ōmu yoku mono iu mo, hichō o hanarezu;
Shōjō yoku mono iu mo, kinjū o hanarezu.

Though a cockatoo can talk,
It is still just a bird;
Though an orang-outang can speak,
It is still just a beast.

In ancient China the *hsing-hsing*, nowadays translated as " orang-
outang," was considered to be a fabulous animal that could speak
and also understand men's thoughts and intentiors.

209. 非規矩不能定方圓
非準繩不能正曲直

Kiku ni arazumba, hōen o sadamuru koto atawazu;
Junjō ni arazumba, kyokuchoku o tadasu koto atawazu.

121

But for the rule and the compass, the square and the circle could not be determined; but for the plumb-line, the straight and the bent could not be rectified.

210. 不萠枝上金鳳翺翔

無影樹邊玉象圍繞

Fubō shijō kimpō kōshō,
Muyō juhen gyokuzō inyō.

Above the budless branches
The golden phoenix soars,
Around the shadowless tree
The jade elephant circumambulates.

DRAWINGS

BY HAKUIN EKAKU

HAKUIN ZENJI, SELF-PORTRAIT

千　爲　群　爲　挫　塵　者　醜
佛　千　魔　群　今　近　般　上
場　佛　隊　魔　時　代　醜　添
中　嫌　裏　憎　默　斷　惡　醜
　　　　　　　　照　無　破　又
　　　　　　　　邪　瞎　瞎　一
　　　　　　　　黨　僧　禿　層

Sembutsu jōchū
Sembutsu ni kiraware;
　　Gumma tairi
　　Gumma ni nikumaru.
Konji mokushō no jatō o kujiki,
Kindai dammu no kassō o minagoroshi ni su.
　　Shahan shūaku no hakattoku
　　Shūjō shū o sou mata issō.

In the realm of the thousand buddhas
He is hated by the thousand buddhas;
　　Among the crowd of demons
　　He is detested by the crowd of demons.
He crushes the silent-illumination heretics of today,
And massacres the heterodox blind monks of this generation.
　　This filthy blind old shavepate
　　Adds more foulness still to foulness.

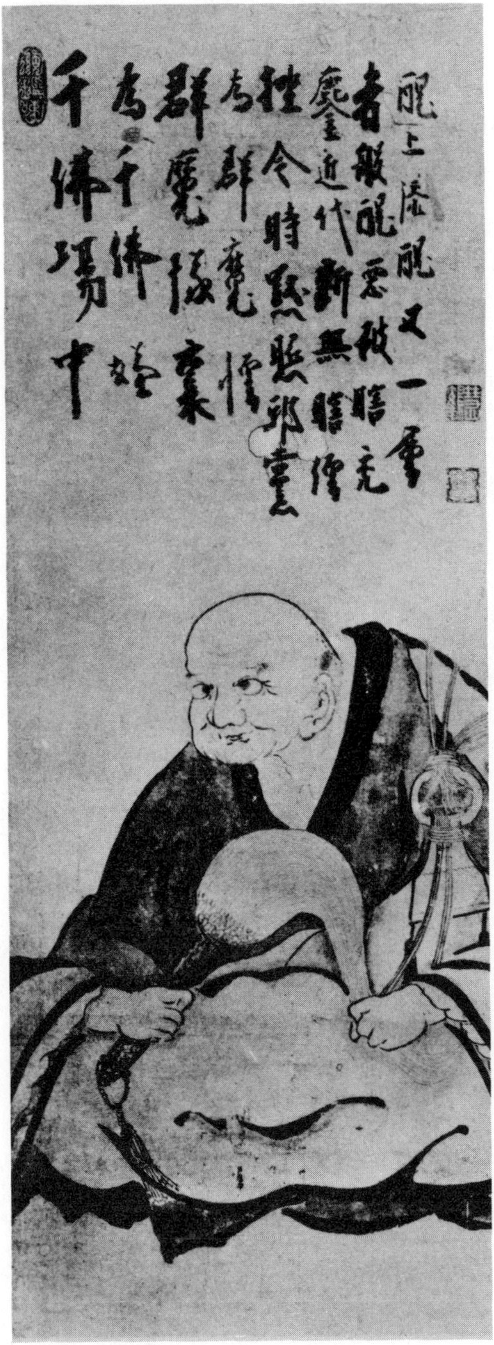

PLUM AND SPARROW

寒梅
的的
西來
意

Kambai
tekiteki
sairai
no i

The winter plum ——
   clearly
     the meaning
       of the coming from the West

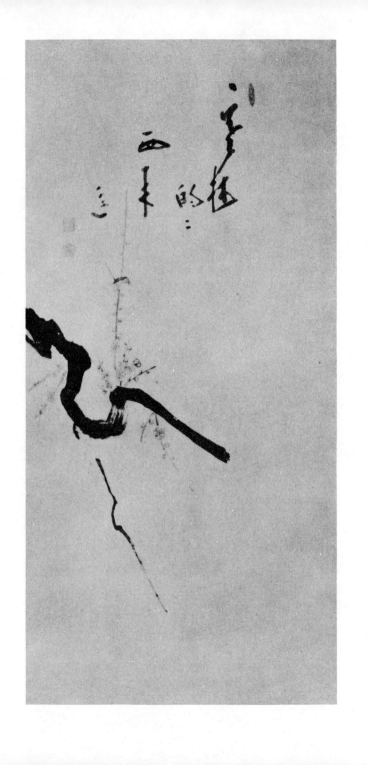

CHRYSANTHEMUMS

悠然見南山

Yūzen to shite
nanzan o
miru

Quietly
gazing
at the distant southern hills

THE BRIDGE OF MAMA*

世の中の　人のうへにも　誰か心の　かけて見よ　まゝの　つぎは　し

Yo no naka no hito no ue ni mo,
  kakete miyo
    Tare ka kokoro no
     Mama no tsugihashi.

Who has the jointed bridge of Mama
  in his heart,
    Him would I have throw it
     across the world of men

* A famous bridge at Katsushika 葛飾, northeast of old Tokyo, and mentioned in several love songs in the *Man'yōshū*.

THE MONKEY

狙猴探水月
到死不休歇
放手没深泉
十方光皓潔

Mikō suigetsu o saguri,
Shi ni itaru made kyūketsu sezu.
Hōshu shinsen ni mossureba,
Jippō hikari kōketsu.

The monkey is reaching for the moon in the water,
Until death overtakes him he'll never give up.
If he'd let go the branch and disappear in the deep pool,
The whole world would shine with dazzling pureness.

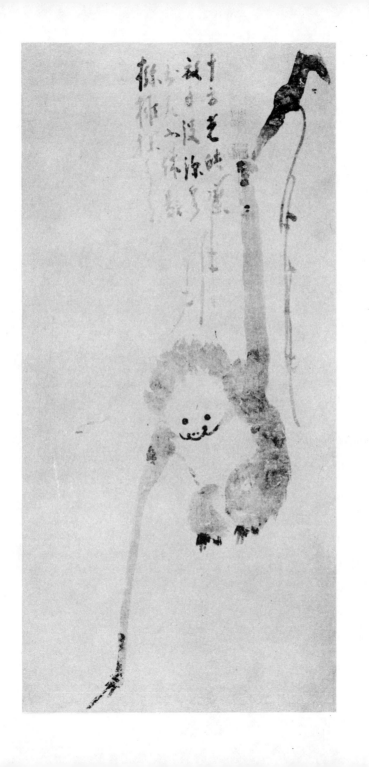

ZAZEN

おう
よ

おぼう　今日は
奇特に　坐禪と
出かけてじゃの

"*O bō! kyō wa
kidoku ni zazen to
dekakete ja no.*"
"*Ō yo!*"

"Hey, bonze!
Wonder of wonders
you're doing zazen today."

"Sure!"

BODHIDHARMA

見性成佛
人心
直指

沙羅樹下八十三歳老衲
白隠叟目鏡なしに書

Jikishi
　　Ninshin
　　　Kenshō
　　　　Jōbutsu

Sharajuge hachijūsansai rōnō,
Hakuin sō megane nashi ni sho su.

Directly points
　　To man's mind.
　　　　He sees into his own nature
　　　　And attains Buddhahood.

The eighty-three year old Buddhist monk
Hakuin drew this without his spectacles.

死

若人 見徹 名 眞 大丈夫

SHI

Moshi hito kentetsu sureba
  Shin no
    daijōbu
      to nazuku

DEATH

He whose insight penetrates here
  is a truly great man.

DAITO KOKUSHI AS A BEGGAR

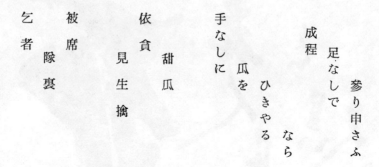

乞者　被席隊裏　依貪見生擒　甜瓜　手なしに　瓜を　ひきやる　なら　成程　足なしで　参り申さふ

Kossha tairi ni seki o kōmuri,
Tenka o musaboru ni yotte shōkin seraru.
　"Te nashi ni uri o hikyaru nara,
　Naruhodo ashi nashi de mairi mōsō."

Wearing a straw mat among the crowd of beggars,
Through his greed for sweet melons he's been taken alive.
　"If You give me the fruit without using Your hands,
　Of course I'll enter Your presence without using my feet."

KANNON

慈眼視衆生　海無量福壽　沙羅樹下八十三歳　老衲書

Jigen ji shujō
Fukuju
kai muryō

Sharajuge hachijūsansai
rōnō shosu

The Eye of Compassion watches over sentient beings,
The Sea of Blessings
is beyond measure.

The eighty-three year old Buddhist monk drew this.

INDEX

INDEX

THIS multilingual INDEX is designed to make possible the identification of all Chinese and Japanese persons, books, places, and terms mentioned in the text, whether under their Chinese names or the Japanese pronunciation of them. Though occasionally the names appear in the text in slightly abbreviated form, they will be found to be easily recognizable here. Sanskrit, Chinese, and Japanese terms are, in most cases, referred to the English translation of them. All persons not otherwise indicated may be assumed to be Lin-chi or Rinzai Zen monks. Laymen may be identified by their capitalized family names. Since most modern Japanese roshis are best known under a combination of their family and religious names, this nomenclature has been adopted here. A short glossary of titles has been appended.

THE ZEN KOAN

"Zen Lecture" (*teishō* 提唱), 30
  origin of in early Zen, 9
Zen Master (*rōshi* 老師), J. Zen tech. term, 27
  role in koan study, 29–30

Zen shout, see *Ho!* and *Ka!*
Zenrin kushū 禪林句集, xiii, xvi, 28, 79, 80
  selections from, 81–122
Zuiun-ji 瑞雲寺, 23

GLOSSARY of TITLES

Ch'an-shih 禪師 (*Zenji*): title for a high ranking monk in a direct line of transmission in Chinese or Japanese Zen, a "Zen Master." In early Chinese Buddhism, a teacher of meditation. In Japan today, the equivalent of *Rōshi*, q.v.

"Commandment (or Vinaya) Master" (*Lü-shih* 律師 *Risshi*): title of a monk who is a master of and instructer in the rules of monastic discipline

Daishi, see *Ta-shih*

Fa-shih 法師 (*Hōshi*): title of a Chinese Buddhist monk who is learned in all branches of the scriptures

Ho-shang 和尚 (*Oshō*): title for a Zen monk or teacher of rank. In modern Japan, also the title for the priest a Zen temple

Hōshi, see *Fa-shih*

Kanchō 管長: a post-Tokugawa title for the Chief Abbot of a Japanese Zen headquarters temple

Kokushi, see "National Teacher"

Kuo-shih, see "National Teacher"

Lü-shih, see "Commandment Master"

"National Teacher" (*Kuo-shih* 國師 *Kokushi*): title bestowed by Imperial decree upon a Chinese or Japanese Buddhist monk of highest attainment

Oshō, see *Ho-shang*

Risshi, see "Commandment Master"

Rōshi 老師: title for a Japanese Zen monk or priest to whom his teacher has transmitted his Dharma and granted permission to teach koans. A "Zen Master."

Ta-shih 大師 (*Daishi*): "Great Master," title for a Buddhist monk of high attainment

"Zen Master": see *Ch'an-shih* and *Rōshi*

Zenji, see *Ch'an-shih*